VOICES OF EAST TEXAS
Three Plays

Based on oral interviews collected and arranged by

Bobby H. Johnson

STEPHEN F. AUSTIN STATE UNIVERSITY PRESS

Copyright © 2020 Stephen F. Austin State University Press

All rights reserved. No part of this publication may be reproduced, stored in a retrieval system, or transmitted in any form, or by any means (electronic, mechanical, photocopying, recording or otherwise) without the prior written permission of the publisher.

Texas public schools may use these plays free of any royalty payment.

Please address correspondence to Permissions:
Stephen F. Austin State University Press
sfapress@sfasu.edu

ISBN: 978-1-62288-908-2

Managing Editor: Kimberly Verhines

Editorial Assistant: Jerri Bourrous

CONTENTS

Introduction / 5

Foreword / 7

East Texas Remembers / 11

East Texas Remembers WWII / 77

East Texas Talks / 113

INTRODUCTION

Oral storytelling has roots going back millennia in every society around the globe. Whether called ancient mythology, creation stories, epic poems, or folklore, storytelling is a way to remember momentous events, individual fortunes and national highlights, the everyday and the mundane, and, most importantly, create a shared identity. The generational transmission of storytelling continued after writing developed. In the 20th century, the ability to record stories merely provided a new way to preserve the spoken word while continuing the oral tradition. It was after World War II that oral history, a research-based process of identifying and preserving individuals' knowledge of particular events and experiences, developed as an individual discipline.

Oral history combines the researcher's responsibility to document the communication through a faithful recording, to transcribe the recording for preservation and access purposes while recognizing the recording as the primary source, and to probe the informant with insightful follow-up questions without interrupting the thought process. As such, oral history, more than any other type of historic research, draws not only upon a firm foundation in historic context, but also upon journalistic interview skills, an engaging personal demeanor, and intellectual curiosity. It is these very characteristics that have made Dr. Bobby H. Johnson a skilled and successful oral historian.

Inspired by the work of Studs Terkel and other early historians, Dr. Bobby H. Johnson began his career as an oral historian in the mid-1970s while a junior professor at Stephen F. Austin State University in Nacogdoches, Texas. Although Johnson had earned his Ph.D. in History at the University of Oklahoma in 1967, his prior educational experience in journalism, a BA from Abilene Christian College, and a MA from Oklahoma University, were equally important, as well as was his time working as a reporter. When Dr. Johnson began interviewing East Texans about the Great Depression and World War II, he proved adept in putting the interviewees at ease and encouraging them to share their personal stories. Johnson's follow-up questions, based in a deep knowledge of the historic context, always improve the quality of the interview while eliciting nuggets of historical gold. He never shies away from the personal or "uncomfortable" questions about race, class, gender, death, loss, or sorrow, and his forthright manner almost often results in a detailed response. It is in these moments where his journalism skills and curiosity combined to create oral history recordings that remain greatly appreciated for their consistent high quality.

Dr. Johnson wrote these plays based on the hundreds of oral histories he conducted in the 1970s, 1980s, and the 1990s. While some may be more memorable than others, each interview provided a glimpse into the past. Although Dr. Johnson's interviews eventually included such varied topics as the timber industry, fur trapping, polio, Stephen F. Austin State University, and World War I, those conducted on the Great Depression, the New London School Explosion, and World War II remain the heart and soul of his work. As exemplified in the following plays, we learn about how national events effected the lives of everyday people and how they came together in times of crisis to support their community. As Dr. Bobby H. Johnson demonstrated so well, one does not have to be famous to be important for telling the story of our history.

Perky Beisel, D.A.
Professor, Department of History
Stephen F. Austin State University

FOREWORD

By chance, I stumbled onto the stage at the Lamp-Lite Theatre in Nacogdoches, Texas, back in 2005; F. E. "Ab" Abernethy's wife, Hazel, was in a play there, and Ab invited me to attend. A few weeks later, he told me one of the performers had dropped out of the production they'd just begun rehearsing and asked if I could fill in. I hadn't done any acting since high school (twenty years earlier), but I gladly accepted the invitation. The production was *A Texas Tragedy*, a play written by Bobby Johnson about the New London School explosion. Thus began my long-standing relationship with both the Lamp-Lite Theatre and Bobby Johnson.

As I got to know Bobby, I discovered we had a few things in common, although our backgrounds differed greatly. He had been a professor at Stephen F. Austin State University from 1966-2005, and during his career, he collected hundreds of oral histories related to various walks of life throughout East Texas. Eventually named a Regents Professor of History, Bobby Johnson retired from SFA in 2005 and held the rank of Professor Emeritus until his death in August of 2020. He received many accolades throughout his career and unquestionably established himself as an historian of notable distinction, with good reason. However, although Bobby may not have thought about it directly, he is also a folklorist.

The definition of "folklore" is often debated, especially in academia. Put simply (by Ab Abernethy), folklore is "the traditional knowledge of a culture." How does one learn the traditional knowledge of a culture—even one's own culture? The answer is simple: from others who are willing to share their experiences, knowledge, skills, and stories. The oral tradition, the act of passing knowledge from one generation to the next through word of mouth, is a big part of folklore and of folklore study. Some people are gifted storytellers and work diligently at their craft, carefully choosing words, employing demonstrative gestures, and knowing just when to emphasize a dramatic pause for effect. Others simply tell it like it is, with no embellishment; they have information to share, and their audiences are glad to learn details of a skill, a legend, a custom, or any other facet of folklife.

Listening to the stories of others and capturing them for future generations, Bobby became a storyteller. He recorded significant elements of East Texas life through interviews of people who experienced them firsthand, and no one questioned the historical value of his work. In addition to recording important events from the region's history, however, the oral histories he collected are essential to folklore studies because they enable us to capture cultural elements that otherwise would have been lost. Over the course of his career, Bobby completed more than 500 oral interviews, which are available through the Steen Library at Stephen F. Austin State University. These interviews—covering the oil boom, the Great Depression, both world wars, memorable events at Stephen F. Austin State University, and black history—provide a unique perspective of a region and its people.

As a folklorist (and as an historian at heart), I understand the importance of oral histories. I took only one folklore course as an undergraduate, but, in it, Kenneth Davis impressed upon me the importance of preserving the past through the art of storytelling. I realized that some of my favorite memories of grandparents or great-aunts and uncles, or of elder community members I knew from my younger days, were stories that would have been lost forever had they not been told to me so that I could pass them on to others. During my college education, I learned the formal process of collecting oral histories, and I have students in my introductory folklore course complete an oral history project, where they must interview at least a couple of people in their families or their future professions. It is consistently one of the most popular assignments in the course. Students recognize this as one way to preserve skills, urban legends, or family stories they've heard and cherished from their youth. They understand how vital the process of recording these oral histories is as a way to remember those who came before them and to retain the knowledge for future generations.

As an actor, I was fascinated that Bobby had woven the oral histories he'd collected into narratives that played out on a stage. In the production of A Texas Tragedy, I witnessed the purpose of oral histories in action. Bobby used live theater to tell a noteworthy story of the past, and he incorporated the words of people who had experienced the events. His family had been personally involved in the New London School explosion, and years later, he memorialized the event by recording the accounts recalled by those who had been there. To date, the New London School explosion remains the worst school tragedy in the history of our nation. During the play's production, I watched people in the audience weep at the pain of the characters who grieved the loss of loved ones or who struggled with the horrors they had experienced. Some audience members recalled the devastation themselves, and some even regarded the play as a means of healing.

By turning those oral history interviews into plays, depicting ordinary people of a specific region from bygone eras, Bobby created something of unparalleled value--to the benefit of historians, folklorists, and anyone interested in live theater. The Lamp-Lite Theatre has produced three of Bobby's plays: *East Texas Remembers, East Texas Remembers WWII*, and *A Texas Tragedy*, as well as *East Texas Talks: A Radio Play*. In addition, the Lamp-Lite Players have performed a few shorter adaptations of these shows for smaller audiences, most notably the residents at Magnolia Court where Bobby resided until his death. The stories are incredibly meaningful to the residents, and I've seen how they come to life as they recall the events and characters they recognize from their lives.

I feel privileged to have been involved in Bobby's plays and honored to consider him not just a colleague, but a friend. Bobby Johnson's contribution to East Texas history through the hundreds of oral histories he collected is incalculable. *Voices of East Texas* presents snapshots of times and places and people that no longer exist—at least, not in the same way they once did. Also, the perspectives presented in these dramatic works are unique in that they go beyond merely transcribing oral histories; they have been put into dramatic form, maintaining the integrity of the original interviews while bringing the people to life as no other narrative would allow. This collection of plays provides readers with a unique and valuable contribution to East Texas history, folklore study, and drama.

Kenneth Untiedt, Professor and Interim Chair
Department of English and Creative Writing
Stephen F. Austin State University

EAST TEXAS REMEMBERS

Based on oral interviews
collected and arranged by
Bobby H. Johnson

AUTHOR'S STATEMENT

This play is based on a long series of interviews with many individuals in East Texas. Since the summer of 1970, when I did my first interviews on the East Texas Oil Field, I have been involved almost continuously in what amounts to an oral history project on this region. In the process, I have accumulated more than five hundred interviews, most of which deal with East Texas. Topics range from the region's agricultural roots to modern industrial development, with side trips to both world wars and cultural happenings.

Many of the interviews have been used verbatim to preserve a real sense of history. Others were edited in the interest of dramatic effect, but the final result, I trust, is a correct portrayal of the region and its people. While the names of some well-known persons were not changed, most names were changed to provide some anonymity. Because of the nature of this work, there will be resemblances to real people and real events. It was not my intention to embarrass any person, living or dead, and I apologize for any shortcomings that might occur.

In the process of preparing this play, I was aided by a number of persons and institutions. First, I would like to acknowledge those who helped me most directly: Jack Heifner, playwright; the late Glenda White, for helping with dramatization; Sarah McMullan, for directing the Lamp-Lite Players so competently; my wife Myrna for typing the many drafts and helping in so many ways; and the staff and troupe of the Lamp-Lite Players for making it come to life. To the Piney Woods Foundation and Champion Paper Company I express my appreciation for the grants which allowed me to chronicle the early history of the Southland Paper Company. I would also like to thank Stephen F. Austin State University for several grants in behalf of research on East Texas and for maintaining the Special Collections Department in Steen Library as a repository of East Texas historical materials. To the late Thornton Wilder, who wrote the American classic, *Our Town*, I express a real debt of gratitude. He showed me that there is drama in the most mundane lives. And finally, to the people of East Texas, I offer my thanks and appreciation for creating such a valuable body of everyday history.

Bobby H. Johnson

1991

NOTES

Technology has changed since this play was written in 1991. The director has permission to use modern technology. The interviews are at Stephen F. Austin State University in the East Texas Research Center, and they are being put on line. Music played a big part in the production of this play, however, this publication does not grant permission to use the music suggested. The music titles mentioned are suggestions, and others may be substituted or not used as appropriate.

In 1990, Sarah McMullan, director of Lamp-Lite Players, suggested Bob "do something" with his interviews, and this play is one example. Because of health problems, Bobby has not been involved in getting the plays ready for publication. It is my hope that community theatres, drama departments, and history classes will use these plays. Lamp-Lite Theatre, Nacogdoches, TX, has presented his plays as Reader's Theatre at Magnolia Court, an assisted living facility in Nacogdoches, and they were well-received. Even though the plays are about East Texas, the characters represent people and their lives everywhere.

Myrna Johnson, Bobby's left hand

2020

EAST TEXAS REMEMBERS

ACT ONE

SCENE ONE

TIME SETTING: East Texas, 1991

(The first speech will follow the intro, which is a darkened stage with tape recorded vignettes, perhaps actually taken from some of the tapes or perhaps lines read by actors, but prominent will be the words "I remember.")

OPENING MONOLOGUE

AUTHOR/STAGE MANAGER: Good evening, folks, and welcome to our play about East Texas. As you probably know, it's about the memories of some people who lived in East Texas during the first half of this century.

Now, some folks find history to be dull stuff, but that's not been my experience. History is just the story of people and their times upon this earth, and I've never found people to be dull.

Here in the area around Nacogdoches, we talk about "Deep East Texas." Now, it's a state of mind as much as a place, but one thing's for sure—the natives of this area don't see themselves just as residents of the eastern part of Texas. In these parts, it's EAST TEXAS, with a capital "E."

People from the United States started coming here about two centuries ago when Spain still claimed the region. Because those early settlers were mostly from the South, they brought a lot of southern ways with them. Tennessee and Kentucky played a big part in shaping this area, along with people from Georgia and Alabama. When you mixed it all up with the Spanish and Indian culture that was already here, you really had something!

It was those early settlers who shaped the culture that we have inherited. The ways of twentieth century East Texans were molded by the people who had already lived and died here—by those who had cleared the forests, plowed the land, and established order. By those who fought the wars and paid the costs.

During the first half of this century, East Texas, like the rest of the nation, underwent a lot of change. For the past thirty years, I've been talking to the people who helped to make the modern history of East Texas. In fact, I've worn out several tape recorders, two cars, and part of my back gathering this folk history, but it's been pretty exciting listening to the stories of those who lived through it all.

In a way, it was a humbling experience as people shared their memories with me. There's something very personal about it all, and I appreciate their willingness to talk about matters so close to their hearts. Things like. . . joy and sorrow. . . life and death. A good many of those people have gone on now, but we have the advantage of their experience. I hope it makes all of us cherish our own memories.

Listen, now, as East Texas Remembers . . . I recall an interview I did several years ago with an old man over at San Augustine. Everybody called him "Uncle Bud." He was more than a hundred years old. He was barefoot and had just finished plowing behind a mule.

(Lights come up on S.M. as he begins interview.)

(At this point music begins—country fiddle and guitar. A rocking chair and stool are moved onto the stage. As soon as rocker is on, Uncle Bud comes in and is seated. When Uncle Bud's interview begins, stage is dark except for the spotlighted area of the interview.)

(S.M. moves to Uncle Bud and sits on stool.)

S.M.: Uncle Bud, I've come over to talk to you about the Depression.

UNCLE BUD: Which one? I remember a bunch of 'em. There's been depression all my life, and I've been here since the 1870's. Grover Cleveland had a dilly in the 1890's, and so did Theodore Roosevelt in 1907. In fact, I remember that one well.

S.M.: What did you do for a living?

UNCLE BUD: I did a lot of things. My folks were farmers, and I did my share of that. I went to school a little bit and decided I wanted to be a school teacher—started teaching around 1891. I taught for five or six years but realized you couldn't make nothin' at that. By then I was getting a family, so I started out to do something else. I had a farm. Then I got a saw mill and a gin and a grist mill. I run those for several years. Made a livin' somehow. I got along. In about 1910 I became county commissioner, and I served there for about four years before I got out of politics, but I got back in it a few years later. We had to do something about that road to Nacogdoches. It was just a mud hole. I remember right after World War I we had a depression—around 1920—and I was keepin' a store in San Augustine, buying a little cotton. We sold it to Moody down in Galveston. He was our broker. Well, as the price began to fall, he required us to put up more money—he called it margin. I remember an old fellah who lived down there in the bottoms, and he'd come in, and I'd tell him we'd have to put up more margin. He kind of talked in a loud voice, and he'd say, "Well, them damn frogs down there in that bottom land, they's all a hollering 'margin, margin, margin.'"

(Lights fade out on Uncle Bud and come up in another spotlighted area where an old woman sits in a wheelchair. S.M. crosses to her.)

S.M.: Good morning, Mrs. Jones. Mrs. Mattie Jones, is that right? *(She nods.)* You went to school here in the early part of this century?

MRS. JONES: Well, I was born out on the Douglass Road in 1896. My family had lived here since the Civil War. School was a lot different then; we went to what we called "a one-teacher school." I remember the one I attended at Old Palestine. It was just a box building with a wood burning stove to keep us warm in the cold months. We walked to school most of the time. Some children had to walk as far as four miles. Sometimes it was really cold in that room, and the first person who got there usually tried to build a fire to warm the place up, and then when you came in you had to take turns standing near the fire, so you could get warm.

S.M.: What was that one teacher school like?

(Lights come up on a "school room" area. Mr. Orum is presiding, and 8-12 students of varying ages begin to file in.)

MRS. JONES: It had grades one through sixth, and we only went to school six months out of the year. We had to work at home on the farm, so we didn't get to go as long as students do today. I remember when I started attending school in 1902. I was six years old. My first teacher was Mr. Orum.

(A six-year-old girl enters and is welcomed by Mr. Orum. Children for the most part mime responses over the narration.)

MR. ORUM: This will be your primer.

MRS. JONES: We sat at a recitation bench at the front of the class when we had our lessons—we used slates to write with. We read from graded books or primers as we called them, and we worked our arithmetic problems on the blackboard, or we recited them.

MR. ORUM: Caroline, will you read for us today?

CAROLINE: *(Stands and reads a portion of appropriate time period poem)*

MR. ORUM: Now, we'll have our arithmetic lesson in grades one through three. First grade.

FIRST GRADERS: *(Stand)*

$2 + 0 = 2; 2 + 1 = 3; 2 + 2 = 4; 2 + 3 = 5; 2 + 4 = 6.$

MR. ORUM: Thank you. Now, second grade.

2ND GRADERS: *(Stand)*

$4 - 2 = 2; 5 - 2 = 3; 7 - 3 = 4; 8 - 2 = 6; 9 - 5 = 4$

MR. ORUM: Very good, second grade. Third grade.

3RD GRADERS: *(Stand)*

$3 \times 0 = 0; 3 \times 1 = 3; 3 \times 2 = 6; 3 \times 3 = 9; 3 \times 4 = 12.$

MRS. JONES: At lunch time we didn't have any cafeteria to go to. We all carried our lunch in some kind of a bucket. I remember taking biscuits with ham or syrup in them. Sometimes we'd have a cold baked potato or a cold sweet potato. We didn't have fruit all the time. We only got that at Christmas. In addition to reading, we studied physiology, geography, and history. I knew all the state capitals when I was very young and even memorized the presidents.

MR. ORUM: Mattie, will you do the first ten presidents?

MATTIE: Washington, Adams, Jefferson, Madison, Monroe, Adams, Jackson, Van Buren, Harrison, Tyler.

MR. ORUM: *(Motions for the students to rise; he conducts as they sing "My Country, 'Tis of Thee.")*

MRS. JONES: It was wonderful getting to learn, just knowing how people lived in other parts of the world and what had happened in the days before we lived. I wish all children could be excited by learning.

(The lights fade and all exit. Mr. F. L. Mowery enters and crosses down to the apron. He presents his monologue directly to the audience.)

MR. MOWERY: *(He speaks in kind of high voice.)* There's some kinds of learnin' that don't happen in a school room. My name is F. L. Mowery. I was born over here in Nacogdoches County in 1893. I grew up down in the area that's now part of Sam Rayburn Lake. I started trapping when I was just a kid. My grandfather would pay me a nickel apiece to trap rats in his barn. I guess trapping got in my blood because I liked to get out in the woods and try to catch those critters. I did a lot of trapping before World War I. Mainly, I caught raccoons, foxes, minks, and possums—didn't catch beavers. Weren't many around then, 'though I understand they are kind of making a comeback today.

MOWERY: At one time I had seventy-five traps strung out along a trap line that covered more than fifteen miles. Trapping was hard work. I had to do a lot of walking, but back then I was a good walker. I sold my furs to local fur buyers who'd come around; sometimes I just sent them by parcel post to St. Louis. We didn't get much money for them. Oh, I guess I'd get anywhere from two to three dollars for a mink in the early part of this century and anywhere from fifty cents to three dollars for a raccoon—possums didn't bring much. The money was important, but it was also fun to catch those animals. I liked to try to outsmart 'em.

(Stage direction: As Mr. Mowery wanders offstage, a lively fiddle tune, something like "Arkansas Traveler," is playing. Music then becomes a little more refined—the lonesome fiddle. Meanwhile, S.M. moves to left corner of stage where he observes a prim, well-dressed woman in her early twenties. She is dressed in style of pre-World War I era—long dress, perhaps a hat on. She is very precise in her speech and begins to talk as she moves from place to place on the stage, carefully pronouncing her words and using proper gestures. She is a woman of some dignity. In background, light shines on a flat showing a town scene of some type—buildings.)

S.M.: Even though East Texas was primarily rural in the early part of this century, there were a few towns like Nacogdoches where people could go to buy goods and enjoy a break from rural life.

(Enter Mrs. Ruby Lock.)

RUBY: I'm Ruby Lock. I was born here in 1903 and spent the first part of my life within a block of the square. I remember living in one house that was right where the present Fredonia Hotel is. The square was a muddy place with horses and buggies and mules and wagons. And there was a well in the middle with a shed over it, kind of a lattice type roof, right in the center of the square, and that was a scene of great activity. Saturday was **THE DAY** in town because of all the rural people. They came in to do their shopping and to visit with people. The Redland Hotel was a very busy place in that period because salesmen—or drummers as they were known—would come through town and display their wares. The businessmen would go over and make their selections.

(On "Saturday was the day" . . . the square fills with merchants and townspeople. Farmers chat, children play, women carry market baskets. A typical Saturday on the square.)

(Stage direction: As she talks, slides of early Nacogdoches are being shown on the screen. If slides are unavailable, the train station scene can be staged.)

LOCK: A big activity on Sunday was driving down to the train station to meet the trains. Nacogdoches had passenger service in those days. I also remember the old courthouse where the present one is. It was a very impressive building. Of course, it did get dirty. Tobacco juice will ruin anything! That could have been cleaned up, and I'm sorry they tore it down. I began public school in about 1910. I got to skip the second grade. One of my early teachers was Mrs. Nettie Marshall. She was a beloved teacher all over town—they later named a school after her. My mother let me take elocution lessons when I was little, so I was in many plays and programs later on. She wanted me to be able to talk to anybody in the world whom I met.

(A spotlight picks up Mrs. Lock as a young girl. The older Mrs. Lock is in darkness. Young Ruby recites.)

YOUNG RUBY:

"MISCHIEVOUS SALLY"
Some folks call me mischievous,
But they're as wrong as they can be.
Why anyone should think so
Is more than I can see.

I didn't mean a bit of harm
When I got hold of Joe
And tied him with a rope
And wouldn't let him go.

When the teacher rang the bell
He was as mad as he could be,
So, of course, he went right in
And told the teacher on me.

She didn't treat me very nice,
And so, I paid her back.
When she wasn't looking, I
Put a great big tack

Right in her chair.
And when she sat down
She jumped and hollered.
Just like a clown.
It wouldn't be hard for you
to guess just what she did to me,
So, I decided that I would be
as good as I could be.

No matter what happens

They're sure that it was me,

And why on earth think so

Is more than I can see.

MRS. LOCK: And I've always been very thankful for those lessons.

(Mrs. Lock primly exits stage.)

SCENE TWO
WORLD WAR I ERA

(Stage direction: Now follows a musical interlude with at least two World War I songs, perhaps a tenor and a soprano. The soprano should be dressed in a pretty, frilly music hall dress with her parasol. Song to be selected, something like "Keep the Home Fires Burning." Tenor could sing "Good-bye Broadway, Hello France", "Roses of Picardy," or some World War I tune. He should be dressed in music hall attire with a top hat and cane perhaps.)

(Music Bridge: Tape of World War I songs played softly behind Stage Manger's speech.

(Stage direction: Stage is prepared for Scene 2—World War I. In activity area, a long table is moved in with several chairs around it toward back of stage. S.M. enters stage from left with appropriate lights on him and begins his discourse on coming of World War I and its impact on East Texas.)

S.M.: Most East Texans weren't interested in what was happening thousands of miles away in Europe in the summer of 1914. Little did they know that many of their own sons would be involved a few years later, and this rustic region would come to know the suffering of war. Who knows why wars start? Sometimes it's for completely different reasons from the ones our leaders give, but the results are usually the same: people get hurt, land changes hands, and twenty years or so later, another war begins. When the United States entered the war in 1917, it jumped in with both feet.

(Song possible here)

People got excited about going off to fight in Europe, and there was no shortage of people who wanted to go fight. I remember talking to one old fellow, Mr. George Hardin, who joined the navy.

(S.M. moves to side.)

(Young men dressed in Navy uniforms might sing "Anchors Aweigh." These young men will be used in the scene with the girls.)

(Young Hardin enters dressed as a sailor. He talks to audience.)

MR. HARDIN: I was born here in Nacogdoches County, but I was working at a refinery down in Port Arthur when the war started. For some reason, I wanted to be in the navy. So, I joined, and they sent me out to San Diego for boot camp. This was in 1917, I believe. We went to San Diego on a train—got in there at night.

YOUNG HARDIN: I was trained for the armed guards. We were shipped east over to Norfolk, Virginia, where we were put on this battleship, the *Vermont*. I was in a five-inch gun crew. There was five of us, and I was what they called a "trainer." One trained it to the right and one to the left and one up and one down. Then the gunner whenever he got on the cross and the cross was on the target, well, he was the one that done the shooting.

I never did go all the way across the ocean. We would meet other ships out in the middle and transfer sick and wounded soldiers, and we'd bring them back to the United States. A lot of these guys had been shell-shocked. They's stood in those trenches for day in and day out in water and mud. I don't see how on earth they stood it.

(Song: "Over There" or other WWI song to be sung slowly and dirge-like.)

(This section should be bridged with music whenever possible. A formal choral group would be nice--perhaps 12-16; three or four on each part. Vintage World War I songs should be chosen. Care should be given to both authenticity and popularity with the audience. The chorus should stand in a formal pose, visible to audience, but definitely background.)

(Lights come down on Mr. Hardin and he moves to Veteran's Convention area and the next scene—a World War I Veteran's Convention is set as the song continues; at the convention are old men, Hardin, Walker, and Byron. Their younger counterparts, from this point on, speak from a spotlighted area. Slides and sound tapes of both music and battle sound effects will underpin much of this scene. Scene shifts to activity area where veterans' meeting is taking place.)

(*Several veterans are seated at table toward back stage. They are wearing campaign hats. A sign on an easel announces that this is a World War Veterans Convention. Some are standing, some are seated. They are greeting each other and having a good time.*)

OLD MR. WALKER: (*Shakes hands with another veteran.*) My name is Ross Walker.

CHOIR: (*Sings first line of "Take me out to the ball game . . ."*)

OLD MR. WALKER: I was born in Martinsville—moved into Nacogdoches in 1905 and went to school here at Hill's School.

CHOIR: "Take me out with the crowd. . . ."

OLD MR. WALKER: I was a ball player.

CHOIR: "Buy me some peanuts and cracker jacks . . ."

YOUNG WALKER: (*Steps into spotlight and takes over narration. Older group fades.*) I was seen playing ball, and there was a scout come in and liked my playing and signed me up for what they called the Texas-Oklahoma league, and I went with him. I began to play professional ball then. I was with several teams throughout the years up 'til the war was declared. I was drafted in the first fifteen percent of the soldiers that was taken. That was in September 1917.

CHOIR: I don't care if I-never-get-back . . .

(*Slow down on second line—irony of perhaps not returning from war. Haunting as though he realizes the possibility of death.*)

YOUNG WALKER: I eventually went to France and fought in World War I. Some of the guys were reluctant to leave their families, but the majority of these boys was anxious to go to the front. They wanted to go. They thought they knew what it was all about.

(*Music Cue—Tape something soft, melancholy.*)

YOUNG WALKER: Once we got to France, we went into reserve in the Argonne Forest. I think it was the sixth or seventh of September when we hit there. We were all ordered to lie down and not to make any noise.

(*Music changes—it becomes more martial. Battle sounds begin. Slides of World War I scenes begin.*)

YOUNG WALKER: Along about four o'clock in the morning, we didn't know what broke loose, but the artillery was behind us and began to fire. They shelled that mountain range for about four hours, I guess, and then we got orders to move up. As we advanced, we were ordered to put on our gas masks because gas was in the air and in them shell holes. We spent the night on another mountain, and then we were ordered to move the next morning. But we had to wait for a tank to come up and get us through this barbed wire; we started to cross the little valley, and that's where it all broke loose right there. Seemed like everyone was firing at us.

(Music begins to slow and fade. During this next passage by Young Walker, both music and slides stop.)

YOUNG WALKER: I'd say it was along about one or two o'clock when I got hit with shrapnel and was immediately sent back to the hospital. I wasn't seriously wounded, but the medics wouldn't let me go any farther because I was bleeding. And, of course, with all that gas and stuff out on that field and everything, you could get infection, so they made me go back.

(End music and slides.)

(Lights fade out on the Young Walker and rise on the Veteran's convention. Old Walker is telling story to the group.)

OLD MR. WALKER: They tagged me with a certain tag. Later on, I learned that I'd been hit by a piece of shrapnel that was about three inches long. It went through all my clothes and cut me, but I never did feel any pain. I was discharged able-bodied. I don't know, it might give me trouble later on, but I don't think it will.

OLD BYRON: How old are you, Ross?

OLD WALKER: I'll be eighty-nine my next birthday.

OLD BYRON: My name's John Byron—infantry. I was on the front line in France at the end of the war.

(Stage direction: Veterans continue to talk in background with lights dimmed on them. World War I soldier enters stage dressed in proper uniform, battle gear, helmet. In background lights are flickering up and down against the sky to simulate artillery bombardment. Soldier is a Mr. John Byron.)

YOUNG BYRON: On the 10th of November, we moved up to the front lines to go over the top the next morning at five o'clock. About midnight, we got orders to hold our position until further instructions. At twenty minutes until eleven the next morning, we got a message from battalion headquarters. The commander said all hostilities would cease at eleven o'clock—in twenty minutes at exactly eleven. About a minute to eleven, a shell came over and hit right near us. It was a dud. And at exactly 11 o'clock, a bugle began to blow taps.

OLD BYRON: You could hear it just like an echo (*voice breaks*), and so they told us to hold our positions and not to go over to the enemy and talk with him. It was cold. Moisture was on our coats. First thing we did was to start building a fire. It was great to get out of those trenches. We looked across and saw the German troops getting up on top, too. The war was over.

SOLOIST: (*Sings "Taps"—the choir hums in the background, or band instrument.*)

(*Old soldiers stand and salute. When song ends, they are seated once more.*)

OLD HARDIN: A day or so before the "Armistice" was signed, we somehow or other came back to Norfolk, Virginia. That's where I heard for the first time that old song, "There's a Long, Long Trail Awinding."

(*Music Cue: Choir begins to hum "There's a Long, Long Trail . . ." at That's where.*)

OLD HARDIN: (*He begins to sing song.*) "There's a long, long trail awinding, into the land of my dreams, where the nightingales are singing and the pale moon beams." I believe that's the way it went. That was the first time I ever heard that song. (*Humming stops.*) In every house you'd pass, they were singing that song.

(*Group begins to sing "There's a Long, Long Trail Awinding." As choir gets to the last line of the song, they break formation and flow onto the stage with others who are coming on for the street scene.*)

(*Stage direction: While this activity is taking place, a lively World War I song is playing, and then action freezes as barbershop quartet sings medley of World War I songs. Lights come down. End of scene.*)

OLD HARDIN: On November 11, they had a parade and celebration there in Norfolk, and some of my bunch broke into a paint shop and opened up a bunch of barrels of red paint. (*Laughter*) They spread that all over them streets, and I never saw such a sight in my life.

They'd all be dancing around out there, and they'd slip down in that paint—women, kids, sailors, you know. One old boy that had a bunch of apples on an apple cart—we just ate up his apples. *(Laughter)*

(Lights dim on crowd; they freeze. S.M. steps into spot.)

S.M.: The "Great War" took a terrible toll—18 million people died in World War I. The United States lost 49 thousand. The level of destruction was terrible, and World War I battles are still cited as examples of the horrors of war. With our failure to enter the League of Nations, President Wododrow Wilson predicted that another war would come within a generation. He was right.

(Music Cue: Group on stage exits slowly to one last strain of an appropriate song--perhaps "Over There" again softly and slowly.) (All exit slowly to music--blackout.)

SCENE THREE

POST WAR— 1920's

S.M.: Once the war was over and the boys came home, things should have calmed down somewhat. But the decade of the 1920's would be anything but calm. In fact, it's remembered as the "Roaring Twenties."

(Music Cue: Tape plays fast, jazzy background music from the 20's.)

S.M.: It was a time of great change in American life when women became liberated, and the stock market went wild. For the first time in our history, as many people lived in the cities as lived in the country. Business flourished, and one president—Calvin Coolidge—even reportedly said that the "business of America is business."

(Music cue: Music begins to grow softer "Business flourished . . . and there should be no music under ". . . business of America was business.)

(Music changes, becomes sad and melancholy to underscore the depression.)

S.M.: It was different in our little part of the world, however, because East Texas was a part of the South, and the South was still hung in the economic doldrums that had been around since the Civil War.

East Texas was still an agricultural region with a little lumbering on the side, and a lot of moonshining. Thanks to the Eighteenth Amendment, which took effect in 1920, the whole country was supposed to be dry. The government called it prohibition, but everyone knew not much was prohibited if you could find a bootlegger with a bottle of moonshine to sell. I don't mean to suggest that East Texas was an immoral place. In fact, it was a highly religious place—at least a lot of people went to church.

(As the S.M. continues his narration, the stage is set for a brush arbor meeting. Members of the congregation will bring in their own wood chairs or benches. The minister, Young Teddlie, will stand under the arch.)

S.M.: The rest of the nation may have been humming the "Charleston," but here in our area, we preferred a different kind of music. Most East Texas people grew up on a steady diet of hymns and gospel songs. Religious music appealed to more people than anything else in the 1920's—especially, the Stamps-Baxter sound.

(Old Brother Teddlie is helped on stage or pushed in an old-type wheelchair by a nurse or attendant.)

S.M.: In 1986, I interviewed Brother Tillet S. Teddlie, an old preacher-songwriter who was nearly a hundred years old. Though hard of hearing and partially blind, he was still sharp of mind. He could remember the first song he ever learned at the age of five and hummed it for me.

(Brother Teddlie is humming an old hymn and beating time on the arm of his chair. The S.M. walks to Brother Teddlie. He sits beside him and turns on his tape recorder. Old Teddlie begins to speak.)

OLD TEDDLIE: I was born in East Texas on June 3, 1885, near Tyler in the Swan community. My parents had come to Texas before the Civil War. I was baptized at Golden near Mineola in the summer of 1903. Ever since then, I've tried to lead a good life. I've been involved in church work, both preaching and writing songs and hymns. Someone once asked me when I decided to become a preacher, and I told him, "You don't decide that." I began preaching in 1923. I remember that my first sermon was based on 1st Corinthians 13.

YOUNG TEDDLIE: 13:4 Charity suffereth long and is kind; Charity envieth not; charity vaunteth not itself, is not puffed up.

13:7 Charity beareth all things, believeth all things, endureth all things.

13:13 And now abideth faith, hope, and charity, but the greatest of these is charity. *(Young Teddlie sits with the congregation.)*

OLD TEDDLIE: In addition to preaching, I led the singing for numerous evangelists who traveled all over this part of the country. I composed more than a hundred and thirty gospel songs and published fourteen songbooks. The Stamps-Baxter Company published a number of my songs and printed my first songbook. They charged me a nickel a copy, and I got fifteen cents for each copy, so I made a profit of a dime a book. Never had much formal music training, but I always had a good memory, and I had a good ear for singing. I attended a few singing schools when I was young. My mother bought me an organ when I was young; I learned how to play it and used that in improving my knowledge of music. Of course, I was in the Church of Christ, and we didn't use any musical instruments in our worship. All of our music was a cappella. My father was a Methodist, though, so I was very much influenced by some of the beautiful hymns of Charles Wesley. I also liked Isaac Watts' hymns. They're beautiful.

YOUNG TEDDLIE: *(Teddlie rises.)* And now I would like for us to sing a song that I wrote. I had returned to Golden in 1907, and while passing the church yard where I made the good confession, I sat down on the roadside under a hickory tree and wrote the music and words to the chorus on a soiled envelope, which I had in my jumper pocket. When I arrived home, I immediately wrote the full song as it is now sung. "Heaven Holds All to Me."

OLD TEDDLIE: Heaven isn't far away, and it still holds everything to me. This song has appeared in church hymnals for nearly eighty years, and I hope it's used for another 80 years.

YOUNG TEDDLIE: Brother Johnson.

(Brother Johnson leads congregation in "Heaven Holds All to Me.")

YOUNG TEDDLIE: I guess the most enduring hymn that I have written is "The Lord's Supper," not because of its merit but because of its simplicity.

(1 Corinthians 11:26) For as often as ye eat this bread, and drink this cup, ye do them the Lord's death till he come.

(Congregation sings "When We Meet in Sweet Communion. . .")

(Stage directions: Lights come down as choral group concludes song. Actors exit stage in dark. Stage is now prepared for a scene describing the establishment of Stephen F. Austin Teachers College. The flat showing the Austin building is placed in the background, podium is moved on stage. On one-half of stage chairs are placed so it can resemble a crowd in an auditorium. On other area of stage an office type setting is placed; desk, few chairs. S.M. comes back on stage to conclude remarks about the 1920's and begin description of SFA's founding.)

S.M.: East Texas remained an agricultural region in the 1920's, and that meant a great deal of poverty. It wasn't that folks wanted to be poor, but they didn't have a lot of opportunity to be otherwise. Old ways die hard. Like one fellah told me, they grew the corn to feed the mule to pull the plow to grow the corn to feed the mule to pull the plow. Times were ripe for a little diversity. Someone got the idea that Nacogdoches would be a good place for a college, and the legislature actually decided to put a school in East Texas. Nacogdoches was chosen as the home of the Stephen F. Austin State Teachers College, after a vigorous campaign by local boosters. The school would open in 1923 in temporary quarters on the public-school campus. Its own building was yet to be completed north of the city. *(S.M. exits.)*

(Scene picks up in the "office" of the new college: several faculty members are grouped seated and standing around a card table. They are obviously harried as they plan for the opening of the semester. Dr. Birdwell is seated behind a desk and is interviewing Miss Mabel Dobbs).

(Characters in scene: Dr. Birdwell, Miss Dobbs, Dean Ferguson, Miss Hickman, Miss Edna St. John, Miss Mays, Dave Whitaker, the black janitor).

DR. BIRDWELL: *(Looking at Miss Dobb's resume. She is standing in front of his desk).*

Miss Mabel Dobbs—

DOBBS: Yes, sir.

BIRDWELL: Now I see from your resume that you are planning to teach in a teacher's institute.

DOBBS: Yes, sir.

BIRDWELL: One of the primary goals of Stephen F. Austin State Teachers' College will be the training of teachers. First semester enrollment is much greater than I had expected, and I need an education teacher. I would be happy to have you as a member of our faculty.

DOBBS: Well, I'm not sure that I . . .

BIRDWELL: I realize that our present facilities do not look too promising—that they are very primitive, in fact. The Nacogdoches public schools have graciously allowed us to use the extra buildings on their campus, but we don't plan to be here long. We are having permanent facilities constructed at a beautiful campus site out on North Street.

DOBBS: I'd like to be a part of this new college.

BIRDWELL: Then you're hired. Now, if you will step across the room, I shall introduce you to some of our faculty who are making plans for the opening of school.

(Birdwell rises and escorts Miss Dobbs to the group: they look up as Dobbs and Birdwell approach.)

May I introduce Miss Mabel Dobbs, our education teacher. Miss Dobbs, may I present Dean Ferguson; his office is in the corner opposite mine.

(Each person acknowledges Miss Dobbs as they are introduced.)

Miss Hickman—typing.

Miss Mays, our dean of women, whose office will be this card table, and Miss Edna St. John, our home economics teacher. This is Miss Virginia Broadfoot, our women's physical education teacher, and Mr. Shelton, men's physical education.

BIRDWELL: Now, we're going to have to figure out how to utilize this space to teach more students.

MAYS: We could build some partitions—maybe wall off office space for you and Dean Ferguson. Another area could be partitioned off for the library.

HICKMAN: Where will I hold my typing classes?

SHELTON: I'll help build the walls. We'll put in a space for Miss Hickman's typewriters.

MISS ST. JOHN: I have been over looking through the old Stone Fort this morning. Since it's right here on the campus, we should utilize it, and I think it will probably be the best place to teach my home economics classes.

HICKMAN: I'm worried about the cold in this building; the wind just whistles through those cracks in the walls. My students' fingers will be so cold they'll never learn to type properly.

FERGUSON: You're right about the cold, Miss Hickman, but I'm afraid we'll just have to make do. What does concern me, though, is the rain. This building leaks rather badly, and I'm afraid the books in the library will be ruined.

BIRDWELL: We'll just tell Dave to have plenty of buckets on hand to catch the rain.

DOBBS: You could keep plenty of cotton sacks on hand to cover the library books when it rains.

BIRDWELL: An excellent suggestion. Now, Dean Ferguson, where are we going to put the history classes?

FERGUSON: The Old University Building is in bad need of repair, but it's the only available space we have left. The history classes will just have to go there.

BIRDWELL: Miss Broadfoot, what about physical education classes?

BROADFOOT: I have arranged with some local churches to use their buildings.

SHELTON: I'll just hold most of the boys' P.E. classes outside.

(Dave Whitaker [black], the college janitor enters. He hands Dr. Birdwell some mail and stands with a broom and dust cloths.)

BIRDWELL: Hello, Dave, we're just about to break up our meeting and get out of your way. I'd like you to meet Miss Mabel Dobbs, our new education teacher.

WHITAKER: How do you do, Miss Dobbs?

BIRDWELL: Miss Dobbs, we're certainly glad to have you as the twentieth member of our faculty.

(All freeze: Mabel Dobbs advances downstage from group and continues her monologue).

DOBBS: It really wasn't a very suitable place to start a college, but the faculty members and students were good-natured during the ordeal. On opening day, it rained and rained. We had mud, mud, more mud and no buildings and not much pavement except around the square.

North Street was being worked on and it was impassable. You had to go to Fredonia, now Mound Street, to town. You often got stuck on it. Old Dave Whitaker was our janitor; he went to the post office once a day. Once as I was walking home, dodging the ditches and mud puddles, he and I were watching the digger getting the trenches made for the pipes. I said, "That's a wonderful machine, isn't it?" He said, "Yessum, it is, but it shore is keeping a lot of colored folks out of work." Nacogdoches was very segregated, extremely so.

It was a very interesting student body. They'd come in wagons and buggies and on the train. Some even walked from the little towns around. Others rode their horses and tied them on the campus. Many coming from the rural schools were not prepared, but they were an eager and lovable group. Of course, we had good students from Nacogdoches, Tyler, Lufkin, and other towns.

I was really scared on opening day because I wasn't very old and had had so little experience. There were several teachers who tried to appear older than they were. I bought the oldest looking clothes I could find. I had to pose to be much older than I was. I had students in my classes much older than I.

(Miss Dobbs fades back into the faculty group which begins to move toward the assembly area. They are joined by others—students, townspeople, etc., to make up the opening day audience of SFA. Doctor Birdwell is behind the podium.)

BIRDWELL: Little did I realize when I took this job a year ago that we would be opening school on my birthday—September 18, 1923. It is, therefore, a double pleasure for me to be here today at this momentous event. We meet to found a school, which in the years to come, will have a tremendous impact upon this region. Boys and girls from East Texas can now come to Stephen F. Austin State Teachers College to study and to become teachers or otherwise prepare themselves for the future. The significance of what we do here today will live on for many years to come. *(Polite applause from crowd.)*

(Lights fade as people get up to leave. Coeds mill around chatting. The larger part of the group exits clearing the stage of properties as they go. Dr. Birdwell shakes hands with a few people. He stops to chat with Miss Ida Pritchett and escorts her downstage. Groups of college students continue to chat and visit. When Birdwell and Pritchett are in place, the students pose and freeze.)

BIRDWELL: Miss Pritchett, I want S.F.A. to have strong traditions like all major colleges. I believe that one of the first things we need to do is come up with a school song. Since you are our music teacher, could you write us a song?

PRITCHETT: I'm sure I could write the music, but I'm not sure about writing the lyrics. Why don't you have a contest? That would get more people involved.

BIRDWELL: An excellent idea, Miss Pritchett. I knew I could count on you.

(Birdwell pats her on the shoulder and exits. Miss Pritchett continues on downstage and addresses the audience.)

PRITCHETT: As it turned out, Karle Wilson Baker, an English teacher and a well-known poet, wrote the lyrics to the "Pine Tree Hymn," and I wrote the music. I did that over Christmas 1923, and the song was first sung in 1924 in the Austin building auditorium.

(Stage direction: At this point the lights come down on interview area and spot goes to singer who will sing the "Pine Tree Hymn." As she concludes, the chorus who have been frozen on stage converge to sing the modern SFA alma mater. When song ends, students resume their casual poses.) (S.M. enters and makes brief comment about the modern school song.)

S.M.: Fred Waring wrote that song in 1940. It was entitled "Make Way for SFA," and it's still our school song today. I don't think there is any doubt about the fact that Dr. Birdwell established the new school on sound educational principles and then built strong traditions.

S.M.: Dr. A. W. Birdwell was Stephen F. Austin State Teachers College in those early years. His private secretary once told me that he was completely at home in any group. He just seemed to have that rare personality that endeared him to everyone that he came into contact with. She said he was a good speaker because he always had something to say. Now that we have seen some of the challenges faced by the administration and faulty, we ought to see what it was like at SFA from the students' viewpoint.

(Each character that speaks steps out from one of the on-campus coed groups that has been dressing the stage.)

RUBY LOCK: I graduated from high school in 1920 and later went off to attend Southern Methodist University in Dallas, but I returned to Nacogdoches and was a member of the first graduating class of

Stephen F. Austin State Teachers College. That was in 1925. Gracy Horn and I were classmates.

GRACY HORN: I was a member of the first graduating class in 1925. My family lived out west of town, and for much of the time, I would drive my father's Model T to campus. I couldn't drive very well, so I'd go straight through town and find a place where I could park so I didn't have to back up. I didn't like to back up. We had plenty of parking at SFA in the mid-1920's.

SECOND WOMAN: I didn't begin attending SFA until the summer of 1933. I lived in a boarding house at 158 Starr Street. It was the Muckleroy House. We called it the "Muck House." Room and board cost $25.00 a month. There were about fifteen girls who lived there. I have pleasant memories of the campus during that Depression time. I remember the famous poet Carl Sandburg once spoke at SFA. Basketball was a big sport. None of us had much money. Everybody was in the same boat, so we just kind of made our entertainment. When I went on a date, we'd have a package of chewing gum and that was about it. Maybe we'd go to the show.

RUBY LOCK: We thought of Nacogdoches as a rather cultured place. We had musical societies and study clubs. We even had an opera house where they had all kinds of programs. I'm sure you've heard that story about the Marx Brothers coming here and beginning their comedy act. They were a singing group, and the auditorium was emptied when a mule ran away outside. As people got up and ran outside to watch the excitement, the Marx Brothers started making jokes, and when the people came back, they'd become a comedy act. I read that in a book somewhere. I don't know if that happened in the opera house or not. As I was saying, we thought Nacogdoches was an aristocratic town. We would say to people who were comparing Nacogdoches to Lufkin, "Well, if you want an industrial town, go to Lufkin. If you want a quieter, more aristocratic town, come to Nacogdoches."

(If time permits singers could do an "operatic" song or a music hall number, an interlude before the Depression.)

S.M.: SFA endured its infancy and moved on into its adolescence. Ten years later, Dr. Birdwell wrote an article in the school paper, *The Pine Log*. It read:

"The college begins the second decade of its history. Ten years ago, in a shack, our bow was made to the world of scholarship. It has been a period of high adventure and sound accomplishments. More than 11,000 students have finished their courses with us. The college has earned a recognized place in scholarship. Its graduates are welcomed in any graduate schools of the country. It has tried hard to deserve the support of its section of Texas and its highest ambition is to go on from here."

(Stage direction: As these scenes unfold, slides of the early SFA campus and events are shown.)

S.M.: Dr. Birdwell would be happy to know that SFA has more than 13,000 students and graduates nearly two thousand students every year. It has a multi-million-dollar budget, and its graduates are spread all over the world. Small pine cones yield big trees.

(Stage direction: Lights fade with spot on Austin building flat. School song plays. End of scene.)

SCENE FOUR
DEPRESSION ERA (1930's)

Setting: Stage darkened, 1920's fast music playing--ending up with the Charleston or some familiar tune like that. Background is flat with East Texas rural scenes.

(Stage direction: S.M. enters dark stage as lights go up. He begins to talk about the depression in East Texas. Music continues in background somewhat muted.)

S.M.: The decade of the 1920's was a curious time in American history. Things were booming throughout much of the country. Business was good in most places—in fact, historians refer to the period as prosperity decade. Now, for the first time in our history, we had more people living in urban areas than anywhere else. New-fangled inventions—the automobile, refrigerators, and electric fans—all made life more comfortable. Wall Street in New York City became a focal point for thousands of people involved in the stock market. Stock prices knew only one direction and that was up. But what goes up must come down, sooner or later. In the fall of 1929, the stock market crashed and East Texas, along with the rest of America, went into the Great Depression.

(Stage direction: As he has been talking, the music gets wilder and faster and as he talks about stock crash, the lights begin to flicker, the fast music abruptly stops; music resumes but it's calmer and even mournful—perhaps the "lonesome fiddle." Then the chorus sings, "Brother, Can You Spare a Dime." Slides of depression era begin. S.M. walks to the side of stage, looks pensive, watches slides and listens to song.)

S.M.: There weren't many soup lines in East Texas. Most people got enough to eat—they didn't have any money! One man said he'd been in a depression most of his life, and another said that the depression just seemed to be one of those things that was supposed to happen. Mr. Redd, from Garrison, said he knew more about the depression than anyone around here.

(Mr. Redd enters and addresses audience.)

MR. REDD: Well, I don't know if I know more than anyone, but I can tell you how it affected me. I was born here in 1902, attended local schools and went off to college for a few years—never did graduate. I played football at SMU. I always told people I minored in football and majored in shower baths. Moved down to the Beaumont area in 1920's—sold tobacco products for a while and then I became an insurance salesman. I liked to play golf. I had plenty of time to play golf while I was selling insurance. I got pretty good at golf and eventually thought I might be a pro. Well, I went to work for local courses as a pro, and in 1931 I helped a guy open up a new course. I never could understand why he wanted to open a new golf course in 1931! The Depression hit that part of the country about that time, and I had to come home, back to Garrison. I didn't have a job! I farmed some, did just about what I could to survive. I had two kids by then—a man will do just about anything when his kids are hungry.

MR. REDD: We certainly didn't have any money, but we were lucky living in this part of the country. There was plenty of game and there was fishin' and places you could stick a pencil in the ground, and it would bloom. You could grow stuff, and everybody had gardens! If anybody went hungry here, they were just lazy. I finally went to work for the State Highway Department making thirty cents an hour, as a common laborer. I was glad to get the job.

The Depression certainly had an impact on my life. It made a much stronger person out of me. It taught me to put first things first.

MRS. PARKER: I graduated from Center High School in 1929. My parents couldn't afford to send me to college, so I got a job at the local Perry Brothers Five and Dime Store. My pay was a dollar fifty a day, so I made about thirty-six dollars a month. We worked from eight in the morning until six p.m., six days a week. I was happy to have my job. It didn't cost much for me to live. I stayed with my parents, and we could go to the Hocus Pocus Grocery Store, and, for two or three dollars, buy a week's worth of groceries. We heard about soup lines and people jumping out of windows, bank failures and all of that, but we didn't know much about that in Center, Texas. I remember that someone set up canning facilities so that people could can food in number two cans. I remember one old man who brought in a bunch of possums and canned those possums!

MRS. PARKER: We had a Civilian Conservation Corps camp here in Center, down at the old fairgrounds, and it brought in several hundred young men. This was one of those New Deal programs, you know, to help people get through the Depression. *(She exits.)*

MR. BROWN: Well, as a matter of fact, I worked at the CCC camp. I was hired as a local experience man, which meant that I was to help these young men who were working in the camp. When it started in San Augustine, it was known as Camp 880, and it was a tent camp. Later on, oh, sometime in the fall of 1933, I guess, it was moved to Center and set up in the old exhibit hall at the fairgrounds plus some barracks. We had six forty-man barracks, so we had over two hundred young men in this camp. For a while, it was run by regular army personnel, and they were pretty strict with these boys. I remember that Captain Lubin was hard on them.

(Mr. Brown and Mrs. Nelson, who is also standing on stage, step back and focus center stage. Ten to twelve men of varying ages arrive to work for CCC. They are carrying their belongings in old battered suitcases, duffel bags, cardboard boxes, pillow cases, etc. They more or less straggle on, looking uncertain. They are met by Captain Lubin.)

CAPTAIN LUBIN: *(Enters, addresses the newly arrived CCC boys.)* All right, men, line up in two lines. You're going to find that everything's done according to order around here.

(The men form two scraggly lines; they are shy, self-conscious, but eager to please.)

I'm sure you all want to know how this CCC organization works.

Each of you will get thirty dollars a month, but twenty-five of that will be sent home to your parents. Your work is going to help them get through this Depression. You will get to keep five dollars a month for spending money. I don't think you'll need any more than that because the United States government will provide your room and board, your medical care and your clothing. Now, you're going to be working pretty hard. Anyone here afraid of hard work?

CCC BOYS: No, sir!

CAPTAIN LUBIN: That's good because you're going to be building roads and bridges, fighting fires, and working in the woods. And every one of you has to do his share of KP duty, and everyone has to cut wood—even on Saturday. I know that some of you boys haven't had much schooling so there will be classes for you to attend if you want to improve your education. When payday comes around, you will come to the office, sign your name and pick up your check.

CCC BOY: *(Raises his hand timidly.)* Sir, uh, I can't write my name. Is it okay if I just make my X?

(There is murmuring among the crowd and others indicate that they also cannot write.)

CAPTAIN LUBIN: There won't be anymore "X's" around here. If these boys don't learn how to write their names, they can't stay.

(The boys look at each other nervously—then group freezes.)

MR. BROWN: We taught 'em all how to write their names. Some of them didn't know what it was, but they were writing their names.

(Mr. Brown and the entire CCC group exits.)

(Stage direction: Three props are moved on. A small cafe table with a red checkered cloth, a booth to represent a ticket booth, and a prop to represent a post office window or counter. Two women and a man dressed in clothing styles of the 1930's enter and take positions on the stage.)

(This leaves Mrs. Nelson on stage with the preset cafe table, ticket booth, and post office and desk for rooming house.)

(Young Mrs. Nelson and a traveling salesman act out the business as Mrs. Nelson tells her story.)

MRS. NELSON: A lot of people didn't have jobs during the Depression, but I remember those days in San Augustine, and I had about four different jobs. My family was in business, and we had to work hard to keep all those things going. I worked at the post office, but I would also help out at my family's cafe at lunch time. Well, one day I closed down the window at the post office and hurried over to the cafe to help serve the lunch, and a man came in, and I served him his lunch.

(Young Mrs. Nelson takes the man's money; gives him change; smiles, nods to indicate thanks. The salesman exits.)

MRS. NELSON: He went on out. I went back to the post office and finished up.

(A female comes to post office to buy stamps then leaves.)

MRS. NELSON: As soon as I got off, I went over to the rooming house that my mother operated in San Augustine. She was busy, so I said I would watch the front desk. This same man came in and asked if he could get a room for the night, and so I rented him a room. He went on, and then I hurried on to my other job, which was working in the box office at the picture show. These were all in the same part of town.

(These changes in job locale are mimed as Mrs. Nelson's narrative continues.)

MRS. NELSON: Well, about seven o'clock that night this man came up to the box office window, and there I was sitting there. *(Mimed action.)*

YOUNG NELSON: Good evening, sir. May I help you?

SALESMAN: My gosh, lady, do you run the whole darn town?

S.M.: Some of the richest interviews I've gathered have dealt with the Depression. For some reason, that period seemed to make a greater impact on people's memories. Listen to some of them as they tell you about those difficult times.

(Tapes play over sound system. More Depression slides are shown. Tapes should be carefully edited to just powerful sound bites of memory. No real long dialogues or conversation. Just brief snatches of memory.)

(Stage direction: As lights come up, a black man and woman are sitting around shelling peas. They'll have a pan in their laps, or something like that. Can actually be shelling peas. Stage Manger walks up, exchanges pleasantries and begins to tape record comments of Mrs. and Mrs. Graves.)

S.M.: Good morning, Mr. and Mrs. Graves. I'm collecting stories about the Depression and its effects on East Texas. I wonder if you folks would be willing to share some of your memories?

MRS. GRAVES: We'd be glad to, wouldn't we, Doyle?

MR. GRAVES: Sho' would.

MRS. GRAVES: Those Depression years were very hard for us, but we got through it by staying together, sticking together, and working together.

MR. GRAVES: It means hard times for me when you say Depression because I had a hard time. I was farming then in the 1930's, but I couldn't make a living doing that.

MRS. GRAVES: We were sharecropping then, and we made a crop on forty dollars a season. My husband would work, make crossties when he wasn't farming—anything to bring in a little money. I often worked right by his side. I chopped cotton, picked cotton. Besides that, I had to take care of the house. We barely made a living, but we got by.

MR. GRAVES: I got on the PWA, one of the government projects, and they allowed me, oh, I believe, it was thirty cents an hour. I was trying to make a crop and work on the PWA all at the same time. Oh, it was a rough go. Then they cut me off the PWA, and I had to run rabbits.

MRS. GRAVES: During that Depression, I learned to stay on my knees in prayer to God and then pray a little bit more, because I know that it was the Lord that brought me through.

S.M.: Mr. Graves, what do you mean by "running rabbits?"

MR. GRAVES: I mean doing just anything you could to survive.

S.M.: Was it hard to farm during that period?

MR. GRAVES: Yes, it was; you could hardly borrow enough money to buy fertilizer to make a crop with. They'd loan you only enough to buy you some groceries, and then they wanted to issue it about ten dollars a month. I was sharecropping on my daddy's farm—working on thirds and fourths, as we called it. Later on, I was able to buy about fifty-seven acres myself—paid ten dollars an acre for it. Made a note at Commercial Bank in Nacogdoches. It was awfully hard paying for that land because the drought came; the

S.M.: cotton crop just wasn't no good. What I lacked paying on it with the cotton, I had to get out and try to hustle to pay for it.

S.M.: Did you and your neighbors around here want for food?

MR. GRAVES: Well, we didn't do too bad, because we could get a little something. We raised peas, corn, sweet potatoes, but it was a hard go. And clothes, we didn't have many of them.

S.M.: Do you have any good Depression stories?

MR. GRAVES: *(He thinks for a moment and then says—)* Yeah, I can remember when I was on the PWA, and I was going out there in that creek hauling gravel—breaking ice every morning getting in that creek and staying in it all day. I had an uncle, and he was out working on it, too, but he wouldn't get in that creek. Well, they put him to picking up roots on the roadway, but he was too lazy to do that. Finally, they put him to toting water. Well, he wouldn't give them enough water, so by him being so lazy, they just made a boss man out of him.

(Stage direction: As lights dim on action area, S.M. gets up and comes toward audience to conclude comments on 1930's.)

S.M.: No treatment of the Great Depression of the 1930's would be complete without some mention of Franklin D. Roosevelt and his New Deal—the hodge-podge of government alphabetical agencies, such as the WPA, the PWA, the CCC, and the NRA—that enabled people to maintain a degree of dignity. Listen to what some East Texas had to say about President Roosevelt.

(Stage direction: At this point the public address system will play several short comments from people both praising and criticizing Franklin Roosevelt. S.M. stands and listens and at the end of the tape, offers a final comment—one or two lines—nothing extended.)

S.M.: Despite Mr. Roosevelt's efforts, the Depression lingered. Unemployment remained high as late as 1937, and it looked as though hard times were here to stay. It was almost as though the soul of the Nation were being tested. Here in East Texas, the people had their share of hardship. It was a time both to remember and to forget.

(As S.M. ends these comments, song comes: "Happy Days Are Here Again." The lights go down as the first act ends.) (Little dance.)

INTERMISSION

ACT TWO

SCENE ONE

EAST TEXAS OIL BOOM

Setting: Music will play at beginning of act during blackout period. Will fade as lights come up. The stage is set into three distinct eating establishments. Down stage right is set with two small circular tables and chairs to represent a drugstore typical of the period. Center stage is a long trestle table which will seat four to six. It is made from a plank of wood and two saw horses. Down stage left are three small square tables set to represent an eating/cafe-type establishment. Open door frames may be set behind each of these establishments to be used for entrances and exits, or door spaces may be mimed, the same imaginary space used by each actor who enters or exists from one of these areas. The areas should be set in a triangle but played closed to apron. Actors need to have an intimacy with audience. A backdrop of oil field slides: which may be changed at intervals through oil boom period. Stage is blacked out as the scene starts. Sound of oil well coming in plays on tape—begins as soft whizzing sound but becomes progressively louder. As sound roars and begins to subside, lights come up and S.M. enters stage and begins to talk about the great East Texas oil boom. When lights come up, actors are seated in each of the three areas. The action is alternately mime and/or tableaux to support the speaking roles. Several extras will be needed for this scene. Stage right—Table One: Melton and Williams; Table Two: Old Man Hill; Center—Johnson, two extras, Mrs. Hope, chair for Mr. Hope; Stage Left—Table One: Two roughnecks (Dempsey will join them); Tables Two and Three—Extra roughnecks, eating, maybe playing cards, dominoes, etc. Extras: Waitresses, cash register clerks, etc. Scenes shift from area to area. Switches in playing area may be controlled by light changes.)

S.M.: Times were hard. "It was a time to hunker down—to tighten your belt." But for some portions of East Texas, the early 1930's brought an influx of wealth so huge that most folks couldn't even imagine how much money the area would generate.

(Stage direction: S.M. walks around—crosses stage, then begins to speak.)

S.M.: That sound you just heard was an oil well coming in. The great East Texas oil field began on September 30, 1930, when Dad Joiner brought in the Daisy Bradford Number Three up in Rusk County. Things would never be the same again in East Texas. For the next few years, a massive boom hit the place as people flocked in from all over the country—like California during the gold rush. Little towns like Overton, Henderson, and Kilgore were overrun with people. Living conditions became strained as people looked for places to stay. During the next few years violence, "hot oil," and martial law all characterized the scene. Eventually, though, things settled down, and folks began to realize the significance of the East Texas field. It covered parts of five counties—mainly Rusk and Gregg. It stretched forty-five miles north to south and ranged from five to twelve miles in width. This was the biggest oil field in the world, and it put East Texas on the map. In fact, this area was one of the few bright spots in an otherwise drab economic scene.

(Lights fade. S.M. exits.)

(Note: The following scenes may be designed through lighting changes, blackouts, background music, slides, whatever the director's imagination and the technical facilities of the theater will allow.)

(Mr. Dempsey, a robust man, speaks with strong country voice.)

MR. DEMPSEY: *(Enters stage at stage left and looks around for an empty chair. Only one seat is available at table with Roughneck #1 and Roughneck #2.)*

Mind if I join you fellers? Dempsey's my name. *(He shakes hands with the other two.)*

ROUGHNECK #1: Help yourself. Whose rigs you workin' on?

MR. DEMPSEY: Work for H. L. Hunt. I used to work for him in El Dorado, Arkansas, when he couldn't pay his hands. Then he made a well and paid us off. I'd come to Texas and had been working up around Van since 1929. When H. L. bought out Dad Joiner, he looked me up and asked me to do some drilling for him. I been working for him about three years, and I guess I'll hang in there another two or three; looks as if the work around here's gonna last a long time.

ROUGHNECK #2: How much does he pay a driller on his crew?

MR. DEMPSEY: He pays real well—twenty-four dollars a day—better than anybody else in East Texas.

ROUGHNECK #1: *(Lets out a long whistle.)*

ROUGHNECK #3: My wages may not be as high as those on H. L. Hunt's crews, but I ain't complainin'. Not when most folks in the country works for a dollar and a half a day.

ROUGHNECK #4: Yeah, and don't forget all them poor suckers on the dole.

MR. DEMPSEY: Well, H. L. is a good man to work for. He's not afraid of anything, that is, in the way of going into debt or buying anything. He'll plunge. He's a plunger.

ROUGHNECK #1: I've worked on drilling rigs all over the country, and it is awfully easy to drill to East Texas. About all you have to do is get your pipe ready, pull the brake up, and let it go. It don't take too long to drill a well here.

ROUGHNECK #2: We got a good crew, and we get along. We can lay down thirty-seven hundred feet of steel pipe and casing in eight hours. Now, there's just not too many crews that can do that in eight hours, but I'm on one that did.

(As this scene is in progress Dempsey orders and is served some food. The two roughnecks at his table eat or drink coffee. Other roughnecks have coffee or beer and play dominoes, etc. Actors on right and center freeze. At center actors are seated at long table: Extra, extra, Johnson, Mrs. Hope, empty chair. Mr. Hope stands frozen looking out an imaginary window or door to the seating establishment of the roughnecks. Scenes shift.)

MR. MELTON: I've been in law enforcement for a good, many years; used to be a Texas Ranger. I've been hired by the Humble Oil Company to provide security around their property. They've had several wells that were dynamited and a lot of "hot oil" thieves. Theft and sabotage are the main problems we've had. Sometimes they tap into a main line and steal our oil and take it off to some little "tea kettle" refinery somewhere. We are usually able to catch those that were involved in this kind of mischief.

ROUGHNECK #1: I come down to East Texas in 1932, and I went to work in the oil field. It had rained so much, and it was still raining, and if you were walking you couldn't stop because you would sink to your knees. That's just how wet the ground was. I remember being in Overton and Kilgore, and to git across the street, somebody had to come with a sled pulled by a mule, otherwise you had to wade in mud up to your waist.

(Actors on stage left freeze—and actors center stage become animated. Johnson is talking to the man—an extra—on his right. He will also include a remark or two toward Mrs. Hope to be polite. Johnson and the two extras have been served. The Hopes have not yet received their plates.)

MR. JOHNSON: The first time I came to Kilgore was in January of '33, right after the big flood, I was looking for work to support my family. It had rained for about forty-some odd days, and the streets of Kilgore, Texas, were paved with pine poles. Right off the edges of the street were caterpillar tractors buried plumb up to the seat and the top of the hood. The only thing you could see was the muffler sticking out. Out in the field, the roads were virtually impassable. Landowners would tear down their fences and lay down the poles to build a road of their own around the mud holes out on the county road. They would charge you anywhere from ten to fifty cents to drive over their land to get back over to the highway. The story was some of them even hauled water and poured it into the mudholes on the highways to make them impassable so they could make a little money with their toll road. *(Lights fade on scene.)*

MR. MELTON: I remember coming into Kilgore at night on about March 10, 1931. Because of the criminals, it was rather dangerous to be on the street at night. You were apt to be held up if you were on the highway, and they could stop you. I was held up once. The hold-up people had built a fire right in the middle of the road. My wife was with me, and I had to stop to get around this fire. The man that came out to meet me had his hands in his overalls, like he had a pistol. I always rode with a six-shooter between my knees, and I just pulled it out and told him to stand back and went around the fire and drove on. This was during the worst part of the depression and unemployment was extensive, but all in all, I think that the people are exceptionally good here in East Texas.

MR. HOPE: I come down from Oklahoma in May of 1931—hitchhiked into Kilgore. The last ride I caught was on a milk truck. I got into town about midnight. I went down to this big tent that had a bunch of cots in it and stayed that night. It cost a quarter Next morning, I got up and went in a little old board shack cafe right in the middle of town. You lined up to get to eat. You would go in the front door, sit down and eat, and then go out the back door. It cost thirty-five cents. I eventually got a job as a roughneck on a drilling rig making about six dollars a day. But that was a long day because we worked for twelve hours. You worked from twelve to twelve, one way or the other. I didn't have much time for anything else. I didn't see a whole lot of lawlessness, but I think there was a bunch of beer joints in East Texas and a lot of gambling going on. My wife and I weren't interested in that kind of stuff.

(As Hope says, "I didn't have much time . . ." and the following lines, he looks longing toward the Roughneck establishment. There should be some obvious fun and flirtation going on there between roughnecks and waitresses. It should also be obvious that Hope would like to be in that establishment rather than the one he's in—at least he fantasizes about it.)

(As Hope gets to the end of his speech, his and his wife's dinner is served. On ". . . lot of gambling going on," Mrs. Hope crosses to her husband takes him affectionately by the ear and indicates their lunch. As she crosses back, he does a take and delivers his last line.)

(As the actors, center and left concentrate on eating, chatting, gaming, flirting, etc., in frozen positions, the scene shifts to the drugstore. There Melton and Williams are having pie and coffee. Old Man Hill is slurping stew. Melton is explaining his job to Williams.)

(Action now shifts back to center stage area. Mrs. Hope is talking to Johnson on her right and her husband who is seated on her left.)

MRS. HOPE: The thing I most remember about those early boom days is the little cabins that we lived in. They were little one room things with an oil stove for cooking and a bed and table and that was about it. We had to wait days to get one, and we were lucky to get one at all. Once we lived in a tent, but we had a linoleum rug on the floor, and that made it kind of home-like. Since my husband works on drilling rigs, we've had to move around quite a bit, and we didn't get to know too many of the local people. But the people he works with here are all very nice. We're just like a big family.

(She stands as she has finished eating. As she finishes the story about the old woman and the gum, her husband also stands. He drops some change on the table, and they exit.)

I do remember one time going out to a well that was about to come in and talking to this old lady who owned the land. She'd been poor all her life and was about to become rich. I asked her what she was going to do with her money, and she said, "Now I can go to town and get all the gum and meat I want." I said, "What kind of meat and gum?" She said, "Oh, just bacon and some good store-bought gum. I'm so tired of chewing sweetgum."

(As Mr. and Mrs. Hope exit, the extras nod to Mr. Johnson, stand, pay for their meals and leave. Johnson also stands, pays for his meal. He exits and then comes down center and addresses the audience directly. As he is coming to center stage, a waitress clears away the table. Waiters also remove table.)

MR. JOHNSON: I started out working in Kilgore but finally settled my family in New London. I've seen oil fields all around these parts, and I've always been impressed by the living conditions—I guess you'd call them "shanty towns." People just lived in whatever they could find. I remember the first house I built. I bought a bill of lumber and paid twenty dollars down on it and when I got the house finished it cost me eighty dollars. You tried to build as close to where you worked as possible because most people had to walk to work. The oil companys built houses for officials and their higher paid employees in what were known as oil field camps. Usually, an informal camp grew up near these official camps, and they were called the "poor boy camps." Times were hard there for a while, but we enjoyed living. I finally got on with the Humble Oil Company. They told me the job would probably last only about two weeks, but over thirty-five years later I was still with the Humble Company. *(Johnson exits.)*

(The center stage area is now clear, and the action shifts back to stage right. Mr. Williams is addressing Mr. Melton as both men finish their pie and coffee. Old Man Hill is also finishing up—maybe turns up soup bowl and drinks the last few drops as Mr. Williams finishes his speech.)

MR. WILLIAMS: Gregg County was a little behind you folks in Rusk County as far as the boom was concerned. The Lathrop Well, some six or seven miles northwest of Longview wasn't discovered until January of 1931. I had come back to Longview in 1928 to serve as city manager. We had the hardest time getting our population up over five thousand in the 1930 census. This was crucial because we wanted to maintain the city manager plan of government. Well, by scrapping we barely made it, but Longview was about as poor as any place I ever saw in 1930 and '31. If there ever was a situation where a community went from rags to riches, it was Longview,

Texas. After the boom started, our streets were so congested that you could hardly navigate up and down them. We had people walking up and down the street with notary public signs on their hats—ready to help the oil men as they signed leases and fixed up royalty deals. People were sleeping in sunrooms and the front bedrooms of private houses. They even put cots in the ballroom of the hotel where the Rotary Club met. Oh, yes, the oil boom was a godsend to this part of the world.

(Both Williams and Melton stand and prepare to leave. As they are leaving change, taking a last sip of coffee, etc., Old Man Hill has finished and walks by them on his way out. Hill is wearing old overalls, a straw hat, and looks anything but rich.)

MR. MELTON: How you doing today, Mr. Hill?

MR. HILL: Tolerably well, I reckon. Good stew they serve here.

MR. MELTON: Mr. Hill, this is Mr. Williams, the city manager from over at Longview.

MR. WILLIAMS: Mr. Ike Hill?

MR. HILL: That's right.

MR. WILLIAMS: Well, I'm glad to meet you, Mr. Hill. I understand you made a fortune out of the oil boom. Is that right?

MR. HILL: Well, that may be true, and it may not, but I'll tell you one thing: I ain't never gonna stare another mule in the ass. *(He rushes off stage.)*

(Stage right and center stage are now clear. Action shifts back to stage left and Roughneck area. Roughnecks exit gradually during this scene.)

ROUGHNECK #3: Tell me, any of you guys going to invest in this here oil business?

ROUGHNECK #2: With a wife and five kids I can't get enough money ahead to invest.

ROUGHNECK #1: What about you, Dempsey? You going to take the plunge with old H. L.?

MR. DEMPSEY: Oh, I've made a few investments, but I'm always a little afraid to put my savings into oil wells. I could probably take four thousand dollars and become a millionaire. H. L. tells me I should do it, but I'm afraid to plunge. But I'm kind of glad I didn't do it because it might have ruint my life. I'll just get me a little place down at Mt. Enterprise—I run a few cows, and just enjoy life.

(All the roughnecks exit. They may pass shopping ladies--speak, tip their hats, etc.)

(Scene shifts to center stage in front of eating establishment. Four ladies enter. They have been shopping—obviously four close friends sharing an afternoon together. They deliver their lines to each other, but also rather presentationally to the audience. They are well-dressed. Ladies should carry shopping bags that may be set down to free hands as they talk or carry only small parcels.)

FIRST LADY: Don't you all remember how rough Kilgore was during the early boom? Why, there was gamblers and all those bad girls down on Commerce Street. Of course, the only view I got of them was from passing by in a car, but they were dressed in negligees and kimonos and there were all kinds of men around.

SECOND LADY: My main memory of the boom times was how busy I was. You know I was a teacher, and I remember that the first year after the boom, I had seventy-five children in my room. I asked the administrators what they wanted me to do with them. They said, "Keep 'em quiet!"

THIRD LADY: Oh, I have a wonderful story about the oil boom. My brother said that he was drilling on the well right behind this building where they were gambling, and there was all kinds of professional gamblers in there. Well, these gamblers ate at the same boarding house where the men that worked on the wells did. They put the bread out in big stacks, you know, just sliced bread, and these oil field men would come in for lunch just off the rig and they'd reach for the bread and get oil on the next piece or two, and one of these gamblers looked down at the bread and told the fellow next to him, "Burn two and deal me one!"

FOURTH LADY: *(Thick Southern accent)* When I think back on those boom times, I can see that it really affected my life. Before the boom, my husband bought a farm and I thought we were going to be land poor, but when the field came in and they struck oil, I had a different idea about it. My late husband used to say, "Before the boom, he went to the post office to get his bills, but after the boom, he went to get his royalty checks."

(Ladies titter and lights dim on this scene. Dance scene comes up.)

(Stage direction: Scene shifts back to drug store area. Small lady—well-dressed, short gray-headed—is seated at table. This is Mrs. Laymon, first female attorney in Kilgore, during boom. S.M. is also seated at table and begins to question her.)

S.M: Mrs. Laymon, you've been a practicing attorney here in Kilgore since the early 1930s. What are your memories of the boom?

MRS. LAYMON: My husband and I moved to Kilgore in December of 1930. My early memories are mostly of the muddy streets and the houses of ill-repute on South Commerce Street. I also remember when the famous Texas Ranger Lone Wolf Gonzaullas came in here to keep order. He was dressed immaculately and rode a handsome horse with silver-mounted saddle. When he would walk down the street, people would say, "Here comes the Law." It was the first time I ever saw the law walking!

S.M.: Was there much crime?

MRS. LAYMON: Well, actually, most all of the crimes committed were petty crimes and minor violations. There was no jail here in the early days, and so they just took people down to an old church, which had a huge tree trunk inside, and they just chain people to that tree trunk. They called that "putting people on the trot line." Lawyers would have to go down and get their clients off the trot line. We'd hold a kangaroo court. The accused paid a fine, and that was about it. I also remember a little flap about some dance hall girls doing a little striptease dance in one of the joints. They called it the "Midnight Rambles." The girls in the chorus line dressed in newspapers, and they danced until the papers fell off and that ended the show.

(Lights dim on S.M. and Mrs. Laymon: They come up on center stage where 5 to 10 girls are doing a rather bad imitation of a chorus line routine. They are decked out in newspapers and are rather scantily clad underneath—panties, bras, etc. Men are seated and standing on either side of the line—cheering, whistling, drinking beer, and otherwise enjoying themselves. Even Mr. Hope is here looking rather sheepish. As the girls perform, two or three guys make attempts to tear off the newspapers; they succeed to varying degrees. The girls are singing and dancing. A string band should accompany them—or a "honky-tonk" piano. During the girls' number a pot-bellied sheriff and two rather weaselly-looking deputies burst upon the scene. It is obvious they would rather be at the "Midnight Rambles" than participating in the arrest. Yet, they sense that this is a chance to see the girls at close range, and so they are not totally reluctant to do their duty.)

SHERIFF: *(In his best official voice.)* Okay, folks, let's break up this little party.

GIRLS: *(Squeal and huddle together.)*

ROUGHNECKS: *(Much general shouting)*

> What'er you doin'?
>
> You can't come in here like this.
>
> We ain't hurtin' nobody.
>
> We ain't breakin' no laws.

ROUGHNECK #3: Hey, girls, Barrel Belly is gonna' haul you in so he can get a better look. He wants a private performance.

SHERIFF: *(To Roughneck #3)* Now you shut up, or I'll take you along, too. I run a clean, decent, Christian sort of town, and I ain't allowin' no strip tease joint to give it a bad reputation.

DANCING GIRL #1: We done ruint our reputations, but we'll be good for Kilgore's.

(All laugh except the SHERIFF. He catches the deputies' eyes, and they quickly squelch their laughter.)

SHERIFF: That's enough out of you, Miss. Now, you girls come along peaceful like.

(The sheriff and his deputies start to herd the girls out. There are good natured cheers from the men and quick kisses, pats, and pinches. Two girls each grab a deputy's arm. The deputies try to look official but become all grins.)

SHERIFF: Come on! Come on! This ain't no farewell picnic; this is an arrest. An arrest for indecency and immoral behavior.

DANCING GIRL #2: *(Comes up and tweaks the sheriff on the cheek.)* Aw, gee, sheriff, too bad you're wearing that shiny badge. You're cute. *(Giggles)*

(The girls straggle on out.)

SHERIFF: Well, fellas, I guess the show's over for tonight.

(The men also start to straggle out.)

ROUGHNECK #5: *(Passes Mr. Hope who is looking scared and uncertain.)* How ya doin', Hope? Nice to see you. *(Hope scurries away as fast as possible.)*

(The band plays last few bars of "So Long, It's Been Good to Know You" as the lights go out on center stage area and come back up on the S.M. and Mrs. Laymon.)

MRS. LAYMON: Someone decided to get them out on bail and came and knocked on my door about two-thirty in the morning. So, I went down to the JP's office and arranged it.

S.M.: What was it like being a female lawyer in East Texas at that time?

MRS. LAYMON: I was something of an oddity, but I had the support of my husband, who accompanied me to court. I traveled all over this part of East Texas and never had any problems. I've been pretty well received most of the time by male lawyers. At one time, we probably had about a hundred and fifty lawyers working here in Kilgore, but eventually most of them moved off after the boom subsided, but I stayed. It's really been a very happy experience.

(Lights come down as scene ends.)

(Stage direction: Spotlight comes up on youngish woman dressed in pants and heavy walking shoes, maybe sweater. She is carrying a sketch pad and an easel and perhaps has a satchel of some type over her shoulder. She settles down and begins to sketch a scene. In background the light is shining on a slide with a picture of an oil well and pine trees. This is Elizabeth Mason, who taught art in Kilgore public schools during boom.)

MISS MASON: My name is Elizabeth Mason. I got a job teaching art in the Kilgore public schools in 1933. *(She continues to sketch while talking.)* To, me, the East Texas oil field was a beautiful scene—the rolling hills of East Texas, the pine trees, and all the color which resulted from the flares at night. Of course, that would later be considered a very wasteful thing—to burn off all that gas and pollute the atmosphere, but to me it was just beautiful. During the three years I was here, I did about fifty sketches, I guess. I have a nice little sketch of the area known as Happy Hollow. Then it was the place where drifters and transients stayed, but it eventually became a very nice part of Kilgore. One of my early drawings is of the main street in Overton where the trees when down the railroad track, and another one shows the famous Pistol Hill just outside of Kilgore, reportedly the scene of a lot of violence, but I didn't know anything about that. Beauty can be found almost anywhere, even in the middle of an oil field.

(As she is talking and sketching, Mrs. Charlotte Baker Montgomery's [artist's name] oil field slides are being shown on the projector. Toward the end of her speech the lonesome fiddle and guitar music come up and are playing as the scene ends.)

(Music begins to play very softly in the background as Miss Mason folds her supplies and exits. The S.M. walks on. Slides of the East Texas oil fields continue to show.)

(Only a few and perhaps stopping on one last significant slide as he gives his closing speech about the oil boom.)

S.M.: The great East Texas oil field remained the largest in the world for several years. It was later surpassed by findings in the Middle East and Alaska, but during the 1930's and '40's it was the king of all oil fields. It would be virtually impossible to overestimate the significance of this oil field in the development of the region. It brought wealth from poverty, happiness from despair, and hope from dejection. In short, the East Texas oil field transformed the area. Later, during the dark days of World War II, the vast petroleum resources of East Texas sustained the nation when there was little hope. Even today the region continues to benefit from the bounty which nature placed far below the rolling hills of East Texas. The area enjoys a diversified economy made possible by the great East Texas oil boom.

(S.M. turns and walks up stage, and the scene goes to blackout. If music has been used, it gradually fades out.)

SCENE TWO

NEW LONDON SCHOOL EXPLOSION

(Stage direction: The chorus and actors representing family groups come on to the stage and take their places during the blackout. The chorus should be toward back of the stage and families to the front. The groupings may be informal and random but should create a pretty stage picture.)

(Music Cue: A traditional lullaby. The chorus begins to sing in the blackout soon as all are in place. Music may be four-part harmony or one solo voice with four-part harmony hummed in the background, but all music in this sequence should be sung a cappella.)

(As the chorus begins to sing, lights should come up gradually but should not come to full. The scene should have a quality of hushed sorrow. As the chorus has finished singing the song, the S.M. steps into a spotlight. The chorus hums the song through once under his opening dialogue and then is silent.)

S.M.: Something else happened in the East Texas oil fields during the 1930's—something so horrible that I hesitate to mention it. On the afternoon of March 18, 1937, nearly three hundred people died in a horrifying explosion that destroyed the junior-senior high school building at New London, a small community about twelve miles from Kilgore. Governmental investigators later determined that natural gas had collected under the building; apparently the gas had been ignited by a spark. Most of the dead were students in grades five through eleven, but several teachers and four visitors to the school also lost their lives. The youngest casualty was a child of three whose mother was at the school for a PTA meeting. All that remained of the once beautiful building was twisted metal and rubble. New London was right in the middle of the East Texas oil field, and word of the disaster spread rapidly. Oil field crews were immediately dispatched to the school to help in rescue efforts. Accidents and explosions were nothing new to these men whose livelihoods depended on the oil fields, but they were totally unprepared for the grim tragedy of digging their neighbor's children—and sometimes their own from the debris.

COUPLE #1: *(The wife talks; the husband has his arm around her shoulder in a gesture of comfort.)*

WIFE: For many years, I just refused to talk about the explosion; the mere mention of it was too painful to remember.

HUSBAND: We lost our only child—our son Tom.

COUPLE #2:

HUSBAND: We lost all three of our children when the school blew up.

WIFE: They were so happy when they left for school that morning—kidding and teasing each other like they always did. Our daughter had on a new blue dress; it matched her eyes.

HUSBAND: We moved away as quick as we could—too many reminders here.

YOUNG MAN: It seems strange that I should be alive and all my best friends dead. I had tonsillitis and had stayed at home that day. I cried and cried when I heard the news. It took me a long time to feel happy again.

MAN: It was hard to go to the rig every day and face those guys who had lost kids. My own kids were younger, and I felt guilty somehow that my kids were alive and theirs weren't.

YOUNG MAN: I miss my two older brothers; we had a lot of fun together.

COUPLE #3:

WIFE: I'm glad they put the memorial monument across from the school when they built it back. I don't miss our Cora and our Jim quite so bad when I think that the local people—our friends and neighbors—are holding them in their memory, too.

HUSBAND: There's good folks here. Some left, but me and Martha decided to stay. Here, we were with others who understood our suffering—who understand just how fragile and precious life can be.

(Two women step out of the crowd on stage. Mrs. Harvey crosses and sits in a pre-set living room area down left. Mrs. Johnson walks down toward the front of the stage.)

MRS. JOHNSON: That terrible, terrible March afternoon I was at home—we lived about two miles from the school—chatting with my neighbor, Mary Harvey. It was almost three o'clock because I had just remarked that it was almost time for school to be out.

(Mrs. Johnson crosses left and sits with Mrs. Harvey.)

MRS. HARVEY: Jack is so excited about his science project. In fact, he's staying after school today so that Mr. Willett can help him with a new part of the experiment. I'm so glad he's interested in school; I'd hate to see him on an oil rig all his life.

MRS. JOHNSON: Our Gary seems to like school, too, but I guess all first graders are excited about school.

(There is the sound effect of a loud explosion.)

MRS. JOHNSON: *(Jumps up at the sound of the explosion.)* Oh, my goodness! What was that?

MRS. HARVEY: An explosion. A boiler must have blown up out in the oil field.

MRS. JOHNSON: No, it sounded like it came from the direction of the school.

MRS. HARVEY: Nothing at the school could have caused an explosion that big.

(She stands and both women go outside through an imaginary door.)

MRS. JOHNSON: Mary, look! There's smoke over the area of the school. I just know something bad has happened. Oh, no!

MRS. HARVEY: What's the matter?

MRS. JOHNSON: I just remembered that Gary asked to stay after school and play with Danny Cates. Danny's mother was going to the high school for a PTA meeting. She said to let Gary stay and play, and then she'd bring him home. It's time for the bus—I'm going to the bus stop.

(Mrs. Johnson runs across the stage to the wings right. Three or four children run on as if just getting off the bus. They say "Hi" to Mrs. Johnson and should say "goodbyes" to each other; then, they run off toward their imaginary homes. One child is a little boy named Sonny. Gary comes running toward his mother. She hugs him to her fiercely. Mrs. Harvey has stayed in the yard—worried and looking in the direction of the school.)

GARY: *(As he runs up to his mother.)* Hi, Mother.

MRS. JOHNSON: Gary, honey, I'm so glad to see you. *(She gives him hugs and kisses.)*

GARY: *(Squirms)* Why are you so mushy today? You don't do this every day when I come home from school. What are you doing at the bus stop?

MRS. JOHNSON: I was afraid something might be wrong at school. I heard an explosion, and it worried me. I thought you were going to stay at school and play with Danny today. Did anything happen at school?

GARY: I don't know. We heard the explosion, too, but we were already on the bus coming home. I bet Danny's going to be mad at me because I forgot that I was supposed to stay and play. Can I go play at Sonny's?

MRS. JOHNSON: Sure, honey, if it's okay with his mother. *(She gives him one last hug.)* You may go and ask.

(She watches him run off toward the neighbor's and then looks back toward the bus stop with anxiety. She then looks at her watch, turns and heads back toward the house.)

MRS. JOHNSON: Yes, he forgot he was to stay and came home as usual. Mary, the elementary bus came, but the bus with the older children hasn't come.

MRS. HARVEY: I'm really getting worried now, too. I'm going to drive up there and see what's happened.

(The two women embrace, and Mrs. Harvey exits.)

(Mrs. Johnson crosses into her living room, but she addresses the audience directly.)

MRS. JOHNSON: I had been so scared that I didn't realize until later that I had run out of the house and left my eighteen-month-old son, Robert, unattended.

My husband worked for Humble Oil Company, so he was with a crew that was sent to help with the rescue. He got there about an hour after the explosion and worked throughout that first night and into the next day.

(Harry Johnson tired, worn out, just coming in after working at school that first day comes into the house.)

MRS. JOHNSON: *(Mrs. Johnson crosses to him and embraces him.)*

How is it, Harry?

HARRY: It is a terrible experience, Bonnie. I won't be able to get it off my mind for a long time. *(He crosses and sits; Mrs. Johnson sits, also.)* Almost all the kids twelve to seventeen are gone. We found one young student who was alive, but he was buried under a lot of debris. We finally dug him out, and he was okay. We pulled Jack Harvey's body out this morning.

MRS. JOHNSON: Oh, no!

HARRY: I don't understand why things like this happen—they were just children—

(After a bit, Mr. Johnson rises and crosses down toward the audience.)

HARRY: After we cleaned up around the school, my job was to help visiting family members find their people out in the various parts of the oil field. Temporary morgues were set up in several different places. There were so many bodies, they had to be hauled in pickup trucks. The new hospital in Tyler—Mother Frances—was scheduled to open the next day after the explosion, but sadly it opened early. The community was in a state of shock.

(As Mr. Johnson finishes this speech, he and Mrs. Johnson and the other actors and chorus exit the stage. The lights fade to black. A young reporter steps into the spotlight stage right.)

REPORTER: That afternoon, we got word through the police radio that there had been some kind of explosion up at New London. I had been working for the Nacogdoches newspaper, *The Daily Sentinel*, since my graduation from the University of Texas several months before. I had seen people hurt in car wrecks and a murder victim, but I certainly was not prepared for the gruesome devastation I was about to see. I got a ride up to Henderson with a casket salesman who happened to be calling at the Cason-Monk Funeral Home. Cason-Monk had already sent their hearse and their embalmer to Henderson where the bodies were being taken. The mortuaries in the immediate vicinity couldn't provide enough embalmers, and so emergency calls had been made to surrounding towns. This casket salesman was also an embalmer who had decided to help out, and he said I could ride up with him. There was so much traffic and confusion that the highway patrol had set up roadblocks. They stopped us just south of Henderson but let us through when my driver said he was an embalmer. I scrunched down in the seat, and they didn't say anything to me. When we got to the funeral home there was a whole sea of parents waiting to go in and identify their children. We went around to the back and went right into a preparation room, and when I saw those little bodies on those tables, it just made me ill. I got a ride to the explosion site with a man who worked for an oil company. I arrived about 8:30 that evening. They already had a great deal of oil field equipment in there—cranes and lights—and men were working feverishly trying to get out the survivors and the bodies. It was just a horrible sight. I rode back to Nacogdoches in the back of the hearse with the body of a Nacogdoches woman who had taught at New London and who had been killed. I may have been the first news reporter on the scene. I am certain that I will never cover a more sensational story. This one went around the world, although I don't know if any of my material was used.

(On "I am certain. . ." the darkened stage begins to fill once again with people. They enter in family groups and crowds of mourners. The children for the cemetery scene are in the group but should be covered and hidden by the adults. The groups are positioned in various spots for a stage "picture." As the Reporter finishes her lines, her spot goes out; a sad, half-light comes up on the mourners.)

(Music Cue: Once they are in place and their light comes up, the mourners might sing "All Through the Night" or another lullaby a cappella. When the song is finished, the mourners gradually drift away and the children are revealed. They stand straight and frozen as though buried. Some may hold flowers, some a favorite toy. Most will just have their hands folded across their chests.)

TOMMY LEE: Tommy Lee Wilson, 5th grade—age 11.

LUCY: Lucy Ann Sanders, 10th grade—age 16.

JIM: James Lincoln Mercer, 9th grade—age 15.

MR. WILLETT: John Elmer Willett, Science teacher—age 25.

JACK: Jack Milton Harvey, 7th grade—age 13.

MISS CALHOUN: Faye Nell Calhoun, English teacher—age 30.

CLARA: Clara Elaine Lucas, 5th grade—age 11.

HARRIET: Harriet Sue Lucas, 8th grade—age 14.

MABEL: Mabel Alise Lucas, 11th grade—age 17.

MR. HENSON: Chester A. Henson, Math teacher—age 40.

DANNY: Danny Wayne Cates, 3rd grade—age 8.

MRS. CATES: Nancy Mae Cates, wife and mother—age 33.

(Spotlight comes up on Billy's grave.)

BILLY: William Todd Smith, 7th grade—age 13. My parents named me William Todd, but everyone calls me Billy. I used to live in New London, Texas, but for a long time now I've lived in this pleasant place with these beautiful trees around me. I'm close to a lot of my friends. I died in the New London school explosion on March 18, 1937. I wasn't very old—I was in the seventh grade, but I liked going to school in New London. We had a nice, new building and good teachers. It was a beautiful day, and we were just about to get out of school when, suddenly, everything just went black. For a long time, a lot of my friends used to come to visit me here in this beautiful place. I could see them age and hardly anyone comes now. I've often wondered what it would have been like if I hadn't been killed that day. I might have grown up, maybe to be a teacher. But I might have been killed in World War II. *(Slide of double grave in New London cemetery comes up.)* I really wonder what life would have been like. But it's pleasant here, especially as the season turns to spring—green grass, the trees, and these beautiful flowers.

(Music Cue: On Billy's lines ". . . green grass, the trees, and these beautiful flowers" the mourners begin to file back in. They lay flowers at the graves of their children. The mourners sing another lullaby, such as "Sleep On, Little One." As with the lullaby sung at the first of this scene this lullaby should be sung a cappella. It may be sung by the entire troupe, or the chorus may hum the harmony behind a soloist.)

(Black out--the stage clears.)

SCENE THREE

1940's—RECOVERY AND WAR

(Stage direction: Lights come up brightly. In background, upbeat country band is playing Bob Wills-type swing music, perhaps the song could be "Time Changes Everything." S.M. enters stage jauntily.)

S.M.: Times were getting better in the late 1930's. People were beginning to find jobs. One local bright spot was Lufkin, where a new paper mill was being built. Dr. Charles Herty, a wood chemist over in Georgia, had discovered a way to make newsprint out of southern pine trees, and although Dr. Herty died before the Lufkin mill was completed, his assistant, Dr. Charles Carpenter, picked up the project and served as its first technical director. The Lufkin mill was the first newsprint mill in the South. It had been the dream of Ernest Kurth, a Lufkin lumberman who had the foresight and drive to see it through. Mr. Kurth and Dr. Carpenter faced all kinds of problems. For one thing, no one in this area knew how to make paper, but there was no shortage of pine trees, and the prospects of turning them into newsprint seemed to give this part of East Texas an economic jolt.

(Dr. Carpenter steps into the spotlight opposite the S.M. and addresses the audience. Dr. Carpenter is a dapper little old man.)

DR. CARPENTER: I came to Lufkin as the mill's first technical manager. I had worked with Dr. Charles Herty in Savannah trying to perfect this process—making newsprint out of pine trees. Everyone thought that it was really impossible because of the amount of pitch in pine, but we had had some success, and Mr. Kurth and his group of investors had heard about our activities. I had done my doctorate in Germany before World War II began. In fact, I was there in 1933 when Hitler came to power, and I once saw him at close range. My feeling was, "Surely, they won't let this man run things." But they did. I began my work late in 1939. We finally whipped the problem of pitch through a chemical process, but some of that early paper that we turned out was awfully poor. But we stayed with it, and finally began to get a good quality paper. I've often wondered why we succeeded in Texas rather than in Georgia. The state of Georgia was behind the project, but we just couldn't seem to get private investors. When Mr. Kurth and his group came along, I had a different feeling. There was something about these Texans. No disparagement to Georgia! But I cannot envision this mill having been established in any other place than Texas.

(Spotlight goes out on Carpenter and he exits.)

(Stage direction: As S.M. is talking a table has been moved on stage and a group of people are sitting around, drinking coffee and chatting and reminiscing. As S.M. finishes speech, lights come up on this group. A jolly woman begins to talk.)

S.M.: A strong sense of family still exists among those early Southland employees. In fact, they still meet every month to reminisce about the early days.

(Lights up on reunion scene.)

PEGGY BYRD: Well, here we are again. I'm so glad we started having these little monthly get togethers. It's always nice to see the people you worked with for thirty years. Here, Sarge, I think you need some more coffee. *(She pours coffee into black man's cup.)*

JOHN BLACK: I guess you could say I was one of the founding fathers of that place. When I heard they were going to start a paper mill here in Lufkin, I decided I was going to work for that place, so I started showing up out at the gate. That was before they even had the thing built. The construction company had already started to clear the ground, and I got a job pushing a concrete buggy. They had a big crew, four or five hundred men. This was in 1939.

Sargent Lewis, a black man.

SARGENT LEWIS: I remember when I went to work down there at Southland Mill during World War II. I'd worked around paper mills over in Louisiana before I moved to East Texas. I heard they were hiring people down there, so I went down, and they hired me the first day.

MR. MCREYNOLDS: I came to work for Southland about the same time you did, Sarge. I had a couple of defense jobs done on the coast--I worked for another also at the ship yard at Beaumont before I started here. But I was an East Texas boy. I came back to Lufkin and got on with the new forestry department at Southland. It was our job to go out and look over our land holdings and decide which trees to cut and which land to buy.

JOHN BLACK: *(Good naturedly and in a spirit of fun.)* Well, I'll tell you what, McReynolds. I wish I'd come along later and been lucky enough— or smart enough, to get one of them "walkin' around in the woods" jobs. That concrete buggy was something. It was a two-wheeled rubber-tire thing that you filled up with concrete and pushed it wherever they needed it. It was hard, heavy work. I broke a rib pushing that thing. It tipped over and came back up and hit me. I went and got taped up and came right back to the job. I needed that 35 cents an hour. I poured many a yard of concrete out there. I guess you could say I knew that place from the ground up. Later on, of course, I went to work for Southland and spent the rest of my working days in the mill itself.

SARGENT LEWIS: Mr. John, your concrete job sounds about like my wood job. It was haaarrrd, physical work. I started out chunkin' wood out of those box cars and off flat cars. We also had to unload trucks that came in; it was hard, heavy work. But it wasn't too long before I got me a better job—stacking that wood so that they could pick it up and put it on the conveyor belt. It took good men to handle that wood. We had to use those wood hooks and throw those big, heavy pieces of wood. Sooner or later, you were going to get hurt. Later on, I got even the best job in the wood yard-- driving a tractor around. *(He laughs.)* Yes, sir, after unloading and stacking all that wood, I just loved riding around on that tractor. I stayed with tractor driving quite a few years. *(They all laugh.)*

MR. MCREYNOLDS: The most interesting work I had while I was working for Southland was the task of supervising some of those German prisoners of war. As you know, there was a P. O. W. camp here in

Lufkin, and I'd go out there every morning and pick up a crew of about twenty-five and haul them in out to the forest in a bus. They'd send a guard along, but he'd usually lie there and sleep all day. They were getting good food and had a nice place to stay, but we worked them pretty hard. They each had to cut a cord of wood a day. A couple of them tried to cause a little trouble, but most of them was just good boys. Several of them continued to write to me after the war was over and they went back home.

PEGGY BYRD: *(As she delivers this speech she stands and walks around the table puts hand on shoulder of one man.)* Well, I may not have had as hard, or as glamorous, or as exciting a job as you men, but I loved every minute that I worked at this place. I look upon you people as my family. Of course, we spent so much time out there together, we got to where we acted like a family—fussing and carrying on so, but I'll tell you that was about the best thirty years of my life.

(Lights go down on reunion. Up on S.M.)

S.M.: The old Southland Paper Mill has meant a lot to East Texas. For one thing, it brought a lot of outsiders into this area, and it also brought union labor. They had only about 250 employees then. Now the mill employs more than a thousand persons, and it produces many more tons of paper products. It recently celebrated its 50th anniversary, and it's still doing its bit to keep East Texas prosperous.

(Music: *The same singers who opened this scene will close it with a lively tune, such as 'We're in the Money.")*

(Stage direction: Activity area is cleared of table, lights come up—yellow or sepia tone to give a fuzzy effect. Sound system is playing some type of mellow music—perhaps some swing by Glenn Miller. This is the intro to World War II.)

SCENE FOUR

WORLD WAR II

(Stage direction: As music ends, the S.M. speaks.)

S.M.: Some generations have to endure more than others. That was certainly true for those hard-pressed people who came out of the

Great Depression only to enter World War II. The United States was just beginning to experience economic recovery and was none too eager to send its boys to die on European soil. While Americans argued for and against isolationism, France fell, and England was blitzed by Hitler's bombers. About the time the American public decided it could no longer refuse to fight, the issue was settled for them. Japanese war planes attacked Pearl Harbor in the Hawaiian Islands on December 7, 1941.

(Stage direction: A period radio is on a table or piano. It should be in a spotlighted area.)

S.M.: Do you remember where you were when you heard the news?

(S.M. turns on radio as Franklin D. Roosevelt's speech to Congress on December 8 is played on the sound system, S.M. listens...)

(The choir and others representing students and faculty file on stage)

S.M.: Here in East Texas, as throughout the nation, people realized that their lives were soon to change. On the SFA campus, Dr. Birdwell eloquently portrayed what lay ahead.

DR. BIRDWELL: *(Spotlight is on Dr. Birdwell.)* The march of time was never more tragic. At this moment, the entire world is in deadly conflict. It is a struggle between those who believe in the rights of man and those who believe in the use of force. The struggle may be long; it will be difficult. In this trying hour, it should be remembered that sacrifice is the road to victory. *(He looks up from speech.)* Some of you may be called upon to make that sacrifice. It is my wish and my fondest hope that in the present crisis each one of the student body will play his part well. Let us all strive together, students and faculty, to write the finest chapter in the history of the college.

(Stage direction: Toward the end of Dr. Birdwell's speech, a few male students leave stage slowly, while others remain with furtive looks on faces. Lights fade somewhat as choral group sings "Oh, God, Our Help in Ages Past," 1st, 5th, and 6th stanzas. Stage goes dark on last stanza. Lights come up as S.M. enters and begins to talk about how World War II affected East Texas. Auditorium scene props are removed.)

S.M.: World War II not only brought the Nation out of the Depression, but it moved people around. East Texans went up to Fort Worth to work in the airplane factories, and down to Beaumont to work in the shipyards. Others remained here to maintain the vital East

Texas oil field. East Texas had two army bases—Camp Maxey near Paris and Camp Fannin near Tyler. Longview had a military hospital, Harmon General.

(As the narrator delivers this speech, he should be downstage in a spotlighted area. As he talks, a small table and chair are moved to one platform. A soldier sits there writing a letter to his wife. Another soldier, a drill sergeant, stands on another platform area looking off into wings. A desk and chair are moved on for Mrs. Hammond. A third soldier stands alone, frozen on another level.)

S.M.: Large numbers of civilians did their bit for the war effort by working at these military installations. I remember talking to one woman who worked in the headquarters building at Camp Fannin. Her name was Lena Hammond.

(S.M. exits, and the three soldiers and Mrs. Hammond enter. Soldiers take their positions as described and Mrs. Hammond is seated at her desk.)

MRS. HAMMOND: I went to work at Camp Fannin in 1943 before the base ever opened. The camp was just being built. At times, I was embarrassed because I just didn't have every much to do. But we got busier as the base grew. I worked in the base commander's office. The actual training of the men took place up on "the hill." and we didn't know very much about that. Later, the base housed a number of German prisoners of war. I shall never forget the first time I saw those men. They came marching through our part of the camp with shovels and rakes on their shoulders—marching four abreast and singing their marching songs. It was scary to me. They worked in our flower beds, and I was always a little uneasy. The officers used to kid us and say they'd protect us. *(Pause—after a bit.)* I didn't know many of the men who were there for training, but I *was* aware that these men would soon be in battle because we were a replacement center.

(Mrs. Hammond becomes reflective. The focus of the scene shifts to the Drill Sergeant whose troops are heard, but not seen.)

SOLDIERS: *(Are marching double time and chanting.)*

> Left, right.
> Left, right.
> Left, right.
> Left, right.

SERGEANT: Get a move on. *(The guys continue to march.)* Quit your lollygaggin'. This is a war, not a picnic. Do you think those Japs are gonna' invite you to a tea party?

SOLDIERS: *(In rhythm.)* No, sir!

SERGEANT: Can you fight?

SOLDIERS: *(In rhythm.)* Yes, sir!

SERGEANT: Squad halt! *(Soldiers halt.)* You guys better fight. You better be tough and mean, or those jungles will eat you alive. Fall out!

(Stage direction: Drill Sergeant freezes and the action shifts. Norman Cooper, recruit, wearing uniform speaks.)

NORMAN COOPER: My name is Norman Cooper, and I was one of those trainees at Camp Fannin. I endured several months of the Texas heat in the summer of 1943. I don't know if the weather records would bear this out, but I don't think it rained the entire summer. And all of us had prickly heat. We had to make these long, forced marches on the back roads around the camp. And we would pass through these little communities with our full field packs, overcoats and even wearing gas masks. It was torturous. Some of those old "Nesters" would be sitting on the porches of grocery stores and filling stations and they would shout out encouragement to us. "Go get 'em, boys." Some of them had probably been in the first World War. I also recall that we were very well-received by the people of Tyler—at least, when I went into town to church the people were always friendly to me. One family invited me home to Sunday dinner and I met the girl who later turned out to be my wife.

(Recruit freezes and the action shifts to a soldier, 30-33, who is seated at a small desk writing a letter. He speaks what he is writing.)

SOLDIER'S VOICE:

Dear May,

It was good to get your letter yesterday; it cheered me up. They are pouring it on us, with these long marches and it's hard on us old men over 30; we just barely keep up with these young boys of 18 and 19. Did you see what General MacArthur said about Camp Fannin boys? He said, ". . . not to send him anymore because they were worn out when they got there." He's probably right. Everybody here is complaining about how tough it is—but I'm sure it's nothing compared to real combat—I miss you terribly. . . .

MRS. HAMMOND: My own husband was fighting in the European theater. Every day, I prayed for him and for the men of Camp Fannin—men who were writing letters to wives and sweethearts—planning for a future they might never have. Thousands of them would be wounded or killed.

SOLDIER: *Male soloist sings "I'll Be With You in Apple Blossom Time" or a similar World War II poignant song.*

(Lights dim and Mrs. Hammond and the three soldiers exit. The S.M. enters.)

S.M.: Texas had 35 military posts, 9 naval installations and 65 army air corps stations. 750,000 men and women from the Lone Star State served in the armed forces. A WAC training installation—Branch No. 1 Army Administration School—was located at Stephen F. Austin State Teachers College. Operating from 1943-1944, Branch No. 1 trained several thousand women in Army office procedures. Each class of WACs remained on campus for six to eight weeks. Ironically, one of the first WAC officers to serve at SFA was a native of Marshall, Texas—Gertrude Beasley.

(The S.M. exits as spot comes up on Gertrude Beasley.)

MRS. BEASLEY: The Army Administration School in Nacogdoches was my first real assignment after graduation from Officer's Candidate School in Des Moines, Iowa. I thought it was my patriotic duty to join the Women's Army Corps during World War II. Of the 19 grandchildren in my family, 15 were girls, so we didn't send many men off to the war. My father didn't like the idea of my joining the army, but my mother encouraged me. I was surprised when the WACs sent me to Nacogdoches, which was only 80 miles from my hometown of Marshall. Our job here was to teach Army office procedures. I personally taught courses on finance and filing. There were 30 or 40 to a class, and we went to school five and a half days a week. Part of the faculty members were male officers—some of them from the regular army—the rest were women officers. The recruits came from all over America and from every walk of life. Most of them had joined the Army for patriotic reasons, and they resented being called "those WACs." They were just trying to do their duty. My assignment in Nacogdoches was really quite pleasant. I lived in a beautiful house just across the street from the campus. We were invited to various social events in town and really stayed quite busy. *(Pauses.)* Being in WACs changed my life. I grew up. I became a more tolerant person, and I learned many important lessons. I learned... *(Thinks for a second and then answer with humor.)* that there was life beyond Marshall, Texas.

(Lights fade, and action shifts to another part of the stage where a young woman in a WAC uniform tells of coming to Nacogdoches—Hannah Aaronson.)

MISS AARONSON: My name is Hannah Aaronson. To a nice Jewish girl from New York City, Nacogdoches, Texas, was quite different. We arrived by train, then marched through the streets out to the college, where we were housed in some of the dormitories. There weren't many students around, especially male students, because most of them had gone off to the war. The facilities on this beautiful campus were wonderful. When we weren't in classes, we were allowed to act like college students. We could play games, lie around in the sun, or go downtown to the movie. One Saturday afternoon, four of us "Yankees" had gone to see *Stagecoach*. It was astonishing for us to sit in this movie house with all of these Texas people in western attire who were shouting and talking to the people in the movie. At one point when it got romantic, someone yelled out, "Hug her, kiss her." There was more action in the audience than on the screen! It struck us as very funny. For the most part, the citizens of Nacogdoches were loving and concerned. They accepted us and even invited us into their homes. I seldom passed anyone on the sidewalk who didn't speak to me. During the short time I was here, I remember attending a graduation ceremony at the college. It was one of the most poignant things I've ever seen. Here we were in the middle of a war. There were virtually no male students, but life went on. We watched the small number of graduates, mostly girls, walking in their caps and gowns, along with their professors. It just struck me as an especially touching scene.

(As Aaronson begins the next lines the USO scene is set quietly behind her. It is a meager set. A piano and 2-4 benches. Extras [townspeople] slowly drift in and are in places "outside" the club by—"but when we arrived....")

MISS AARONSON: *(Pauses.)* Another humorous story I should tell concerns the opening of a USO type club. The city had worked very hard to open this club for us and for other soldiers passing through town. We were all instructed to go down for the opening ceremonies, but when we arrived, it was so crowded in front of the club that we could hardly get in. Everybody from miles around seemed to be present. There were farmers dressed in their best overalls, along with a lot of townspeople. We had to politely push our way inside, and once we got in, there wasn't much to do. There was a piano and a record player, but no men to dance with. Outside, the local people just looked at us through the windows. We decided to put on a show for them, so we started singing and dancing with one another. We sang nearly all the songs we knew.

(Stage direction: As she describes the scene, a crowd of local citizens—men in cowboy hats and boots and women dressed suitably are gawking at the WACS who wander on stage and enter the club. At this point a trio of WACS or one soloist will sing a verse of a song or two, perhaps some Andrew Sisters type things, such as "Boogie Woogie Bugle Boy," "Don't Sit Under the Apple Tree," "Deep in the Heart of Texas," "You are My Sunshine" and that type of thing. When the song ends, Miss Aaronson walks toward the center of the stage and concludes the scene with a brief comment. The people in the crowd freeze. When Aaronson finishes her last line, they clear the USO props and exit.)

MISS AARONSON: I was in the service for three years. One of my fondest memories is of the Texas hospitality.

(Aaronson exits: The stage is clear. Lights come up on Dr. Birdwell giving some instructions to his secretary.)

DR. BIRDWELL: Miss Spears, be sure to remind those people over at the *Pine Log* office to send a copy of the student newspaper to every SFA student who is off in the war.

(Meanwhile elsewhere on the stage spotlight focuses on a sailor dressed in white garb who stands with a handful of newspapers. He tells about the joy of receiving news from home.)

HAPPY SAILOR: Gee whiz! I got a whole year's worth of the *Pine Log* at one time. *(He holds an armful of papers.)* A few of them look a little worse for the wear. Looks like this one's been burned. Maybe the ship got hit. I'm gonna take these things to my bunk and put 'em in order and read every page. *(He looks off into the distance.)* Boy, I sure am a long way from Nacogdoches, Texas. *(Lights fade as music comes up.)*

S.M.: A lot of people found themselves going places during the war. An East Texas bus line played an important role during those troubled years. Since gasoline was scarce, people rode the bus virtually everywhere. Airline Motor Coaches served most of East Texas then, especially the runs from Houston to Shreveport and from Tyler to Beaumont. Their headquarters was right here in Nacogdoches.

(Stage direction: young woman enters stage right. She goes to center and speaks.)

BETTY MCKENZIE: I'm Betty McKenzie; I worked as a ticket agent for Airline. I'll tell you one thing—those busses were full. People stood in the aisles and sat on their suitcases. Service men got the first seats—that was company policy. A lot of busses came in about 1:30 in the morning, and since I lived across the street from the station I would sometimes go over and give the night crew a hand. It seemed like everyone was going somewhere.

(Stage direction: scene shifts stage left to bus station in Nacogdoches. Betty walks over and gets behind ticket counter. A short line of customers--young woman, older woman, and young airman. Each has suitcase. Small talk ensues as patrons buy tickets. Lights up on ticket counter moved on stage.)

TICKET AGENT: Where are ya' going, honey?

YOUNG WOMAN: I need a ticket to Mineral Wells. I'm going to see my husband. He's stationed at Camp Walters. They're about to ship him out.

AGENT: I know how you feel—my brother's over at Fort Benning in Georgia. *(She sells ticket to woman who moves away.)*

OLDER WOMAN: *(meekly)* Could I but a ticket to Beaumont? My husband is working down there at the shipyard.

AGENT: Sure, we've got an extra running tonight. It's due in here any minute. Is that one way or round trip?

WOMAN: One way. He's found us a little garage apartment down there. I hate to move, but we've been apart so long. *(She takes ticket, pays agent and moves on.)*

AGENT: How about you, soldier? Where are you going? *(Soldier steps up to counter.)*

AIRMAN: Give me a one-way to Shreveport, please. I've got to get back to Barksdale Field quick. My leave's almost up. I guess I'll be going overseas soon. I hope the war lasts until I can get there.

AGENT: Well, we'll do our best to get you to Shreveport, but you may have to sit in the aisle. Good luck.

(Lights down as perhaps "Sentimental Journey" or something similar comes up on sound system.)

(Stage direction: Stage is clear. A nice chair is brought to down left. Mrs. Edwards enters and addresses the audience. Action returns to interview area where middle aged woman sits at table reminiscing about the home front in East Texas. As she speaks, slides of home front scenes will be shown. This is Sara Edwards.)

MRS. EDWARDS: I was 14 years old when World War II began—a sophomore at Nacogdoches High School. I remember coming out of the picture show that Sunday afternoon in December and hearing about the Japanese attack on Pearl Harbor. An extra edition of *The Daily Sentinel* was already on the streets. The next day at school, we listened to President Roosevelt's speech and the school band played "The Star-Spangled Banner." There wasn't a dry eye in the whole place. *(Mrs. Edwards exits left and sits in chair.)* The war was exciting to school kids. We hadn't yet begun to understand its meaning, but we got involved in all kinds of patriotic activities, like collecting scrap metal. We had a scrap metal drive at school. It was so successful that the whole campus was filled with junk, including old rusted jalopies and even parts of an old locomotive! My homeroom won the prize for collecting the most metal. The war began to come home to us as our friends went off. The class of 1939 lost several boys. The class had 25 boys on its football team—7 were killed. I remember being in the principal's office one day when word came that one of our former students had been killed. One of the teachers was in the office and she began to cry, and the principal, Mr. Chambers, just went back into his office and closed the door.

(Stage directions: Young Mrs. Edwards appears behind her older self. Mrs. Edwards and Young Mrs. Edwards begin speaking the next lines simultaneously. At ". . . he didn't even get to stay for graduation," Young Mrs. Edwards takes over. Mrs. Edwards stays on stage watching her younger self.)

MRS. EDWARDS and YOUNG MRS. EDWARDS: When we were about to graduate in the spring of 1944, one of our classmates, Oliver Baker, was being taken into the service.

YOUNG MRS. EDWARDS: He didn't even get to stay for graduation. My best friend, Mary Ann, was his girlfriend and we decided to do something special for them. We went with them down to the train station to see him off. . .

(Stage direction: Young Mrs. Edwards crosses back and becomes a part of this scene. A small group of high school students enter from stage right. Oliver and Mary Ann are holding hands. They pull a little apart from the rest of the group to say their good-byes. The other students whisper and mime taking up a collection. They are secretive and in high spirits.)

OLIVER: Gee, Mary Ann—you know I'm going to miss you.

MARY ANN: I'll write to you every day.

OLIVER: I'm really keen about the picture you gave me. That picture will always be with me wherever I go.

(Girl #2 rushes off left. She has the money the group has collected. She is going into the station to buy a ticket for Mary Ann.)

MARY ANN: Oh, Oliver, I can't stand this.

(They hug and are joined by the rest of the group.)

BOY #1: Good luck, old man! Tell that sergeant who inducts you, that you want to go in as a general. *(They all laugh.)*

GIRL #1: You just be sure you don't forget us.

GIRL #3: All you boys who are leaving better come back so we can have some dates again.

GIRL #2: *(Rushes back on stage.)* I got it! I got it!

YOUNG MRS. EDWARDS: Mary Ann, we bought you a round trip ticket to Houston. You can go with Oliver and see him off. *(Squeals all around.)*

MARY ANN: This is wonderful. *(The impact of what she is contemplating dawns on her.)* But what will my parents say?

YOUNG MRS. EDWARDS: Don't worry! We'll explain everything. Just be sure you're back by graduation. *(They all laugh.)*

(A train whistle sounds—an "All Aboard" is heard. Mary Ann and Oliver rush out to get on train—off left. The others stand waving good-bye; then, they exit right. Young Edwards stays on stage. After Mrs. Edwards line, Young Mrs. Edwards crosses down to audience.)

MRS. EDWARDS: It was really very innocent because his aunt and uncle met them at the train in Houston, and they spent the night with his aunt and uncle. They never were unchaperoned.

YOUNG MRS. EDWARDS: *(Crosses to spotlight area right, addressing the audience.)* I guess we didn't explain things very well because when Mary Ann got back, her parents grounded her for a month. They wouldn't allow her to talk on the telephone or communicate with any of us. I thought it was the most romantic event that happened to anyone I knew during the entire war. *(Lights out on Young Edwards.)*

MRS. EDWARDS: We had a ritual that we went through when one of our friends went off to war. A couple of days before, we'd go to Fern Lake and have an all-day picnic. Then, the night before they left, we gave a party with their family. The next day, we'd all accompany them to the train station or the bus station to see them off. Those were extremely emotional partings. We were very lucky—all those boys came back.

YOUNG MRS. EDWARDS: *(Takes over the scene.)* I went to SFA in the fall of 1944 and it was a pretty drab place. There were only 350 students there and only 25 were boys. They were either high school graduates too young to go to war or 4-F's. At the dances in the social hall, girls danced with girls. They all lined up to tag in on what few boys there were. My daddy was not happy when the WACs came to SFA! He was the basketball coach, and he said that we were the only school in the Lone Star Conference that didn't get some kind of naval unit with men who could play basketball. Instead, we got WACs! My social club, the Pine Burrs, often rode a school bus to Harmon Hospital in Longview to entertain boys who had been wounded. We sang songs and did skits for them. We were scared to death; those guys encouraged us more than we did them. We also wrote letters to all the boys overseas. We gathered at friends' houses and wrote letters to our favorite GI Joe's all over the world. "Hey, Mom, we're meeting at Mary Ann's tonight to write letters. See you around 9:30." *(She exits.)*

MRS. EDWARDS: Sometimes it seemed like the war would never end, but it did, and it didn't take long for things to get back to normal. By 1946, when all the veterans were coming home, the enrollment at the college had more than doubled. The ratio of men was 7 to 1. We were having dances where guys were standing in stag lines waiting to dance with the girls. It was wonderful.

S.M.: *(A little out of breath.) (Dance music down. Appropriate music plays under this speech.)* Life went on in East Texas during the war, but the war seemed endless. People hoped and prayed that those they loved would be spared. Each individual prayer was multiplied by millions of others. Families placed small blue flags in their windows to show that one of their own was serving his country. Too many East Texas windows displayed gold stars—a symbol that a family member had been killed in the line of duty.

Finally, it was over! First, Germany surrendered in the spring of 1945. Japan held on until summer. President Truman made a fearful decision to use the atomic bomb. But Truman had been right—the ultimate weapon brought Japan to its knees.

(S.M. is silent: Farm couple enters and sits in chairs on stage right. A mother and three children are grouped around the chair on the left. Mrs. Hammond sits at her typewriter. A soloist or two—one male, one female—stands on center level.)

S.M.: The troops came home to the greatest homecoming celebration ever seen. A gigantic family reunion of the whole country. Family after family was reunited.

(Stage directions: As S.M. concludes his speech the soloist(s) begin to sing an appropriate World War II song: "Kiss Me Once" . . . It's Been a Long, Long Time." "Sentimental Journey," or "You'll Never Know Just How Much I Miss You." A young serviceman enters and is reunited with his farmer parents on stage left. A young Mr. Hammond returns to his wife. He lifts her up, kisses her, and they begin to dance center stage to the music. Lights are somewhat dim, and the scene ends with song ending and lights fading. Stage does dark.)

FINALE: *(Lights come back up, music is playing, and seven characters reappear across the stage. S.M. needs to be active, perhaps greeting the characters with a nod or wave. Each character then speaks.)*

M. L. MOWERY: It was fun to catch those animals. I like trying to outsmart 'em!

MRS. MATTIE JONES: It was wonderful learning back then!

OLD MR. HARDIN: And we ate up every one of them apples!

MR. GRAVES: So, they just made him a boss man!

MR. REDD: The depression made a stronger man out of me.

FOURTH LADY: After the boom, he went to pick up his royalty checks!

MRS. BEASLEY: Being in the WACS changed my life. I grew up.

MRS. EDWARDS: The ratio was seven to one. It was wonderful!

(S.M. saunters in and makes last statement.)

S.M.: And that's how East Texas remembers!

EAST TEXAS REMEMBERS WORLD WAR II

by
Bobby H. Johnson

AUTHOR'S STATEMENT

This play is based on a series of oral history interviews compiled over the past several years. It was inspired by my earlier play, *East Texas Remembers*, written and performed in the spring of 1991.

During the past few years, I have interviewed nearly a hundred persons, mostly from East Texas, concerning their memories of World War II. Most of the names have been changed because this is a dramatized version of the interviews. There is no intention to embarrass any person, living or dead, by the presentation of this work, which is intended to portray the history of this region.

A briefer version was presented in the spring of 1992 during a World War II symposium at Stephen F. Austin State University. The Lamp-Lite Players of Nacogdoches ably performed on that occasion, and I express by appreciation to them. In addition, I would like to thank my wife, Myrna E. Johnson, for typing the manuscript, and Sarah McMullan, director of the Lamp-Lite Playhouse, for her constant encouragement.

Bobby H. Johnson

Nacogdoches, Texas

February 8, 1993

NOTES

Technology has changed since this play was written in 1992. The director has permission to use modern technology. The interviews are at Stephen F. Austin State University in the East Texas Research Center, and they are being put on line. Music played a big part in the production of this play, however, this publication does not grant permission to use the music suggested. The music titles mentioned are suggestions, and others may be substituted or not used as appropriate.

In 1990, Sarah McMullan, director of Lamp-Lite Players, suggested Bob "do something" with his interviews, and this play is one example. Because of health problems, Bobby has not been involved in getting the plays ready for publication. It is my hope that community theatres, drama departments, and history classes will use these plays, sometimes as community service. Lamp-Lite Theatre, Nacogdoches, TX, has presented his plays as Reader's Theatre at Magnolia Court, an assisted living facility in Nacogdoches, and they were well-received. Even though the plays are about East Texas, the characters represent people and their lives everywhere.

Myrna Johnson, Bobby's left hand

2020

EAST TEXAS REMEMBERS WORLD WAR II

ACT I
EAST TEXAS TODAY (1993)

INTRODUCTION:

(Stage set with large movie screen as back drop. On both sides, two flats painted black, decorated with World War II posters, perhaps a Coke sign, etc. A small table in middle, with old cathedral-type radio sitting on it with a few World War II or 1940's artifacts. Cut out cardboard picture of Betty Grable located somewhere on stage. Elsewhere on stage, are platforms for dramatic effectiveness and a carousel for various scene changes. Sound system off to one side where operator can be inconspicuous.)

Tape recorded voices will deliver vignettes, after several minutes of WWII era music plays, as crowd gathers. Vignettes taken from tape recordings—should be clear and audible. Actors will sit on chairs or stools located on both sides in front of flats, with S.M.'s stool set off a little. Three podiums arranged in front of chairs. Play will be done in readers' theater format.

Lighting will be overhead spots, but not so bright as to ruin slides on screen. Appropriate slides will portray various war scenes. They will be shown throughout, but a few slides will remain on screen while some speeches are delivered. House lights down.

A series of speeches will be delivered with introductions and commentary by S.M.

Stage direction: lights down. Music fades. Lights up on carousel set with table and two chairs. S.M. is conducting interview with a man about WWII. S.M. gets up and walks center stage to introduce play.)

AUTHOR/STAGE MANAGER: I appreciate your agreeing to talk with me about World War II, Mr. Wingo. I've been doing these interviews for several years now. It's a good way to preserve a little history about events like the second World War. Tell me, where were you when the war began?

FRED WINGO: I was there when it started. Actually, I was on a destroyer about two hundred miles off of Pearl Harbor. We were doing escort duty for the aircraft carrier *Enterprise*. We got back into Pearl the next day—December 8—and it was a mess. Everything was still on fire, a good part of the fleet was sunk, and we knew that something big had started. We put out to sea almost immediately and stayed on patrol for the rest of the war. My ship was involved in a number of campaigns against the Japanese. I was a yeoman, which meant that I did all the ship's clerical duties, but I had a battle station, too. I was a spotter on a 5-inch gun crew—that was my battle station—and we saw a lot of combat. I was on that ship 'til the war ended, but you know, we never had a man killed. This little reunion here in Nacogdoches is the first time I've seen most of these guys since World War II ended.

(At this point, lights go down on carrousel. S.M. gets up and walks to his stool where he begins his first speech.)

S.M.: Good evening, folks. I'd like to welcome you to this little program on World War II. It's been fifty years since our nation first became involved in the greatest event of our time. In looking back on that conflict, some people tend to see it as a "good" war. Now, I'd be the first to admit that someone had to stop a madman like Hitler, but I'll be darned if I'm going to call anything that killed 50 million people "good." It was just one of those times in history when a nasty job had to be done. Historians tell us that this war grew out of the failures of the first World War a generation earlier. Regardless of the causes, World War II defined the first half of the 1940's, and it's continued to shape world events ever since. In fact, we're only now seeing the concluding effects of that traumatic conflict.

East Texas—our "little corner of the world"—played a big role in that war. Some three-quarters of a million Texans served in the war, and countless others were involved in home front efforts. A good many of those were from East Texas. Some people say that we couldn't have won the war if it hadn't been for the great East Texas Oil Field. When you add in the shipyards down on the coast and all the airplane factories up around Fort Worth, you begin to get the picture—not to mention all the agricultural and forest related production. Two large training bases were located in East Texas—Camp Maxey up at Paris and Camp Fannin near Tyler. Harmon Hospital in Longview also did its part. We even had two military training schools right here in this area—a Women's Army

Corps Unit was in Nacogdoches and a Clerical Training unit over at Sam Houston in Huntsville. All of this brought the war home to East Texas.

Like I said, for the past several years, I've been tape recording the memories of those involved in that war. Through the magic of this little gadget (points to tape recorder), those memories will remain long after we're gone . . . I was just a kid not far from here during those years, and I have a few memories of my own. I'll never forget the troop trains that passed through Overton, Texas. It was all very exciting! I think I saw every war movie, beginning with Bob Hope in *Caught in the Draft*. I fell in love with several movie stars, including the beautiful Joan Leslie, who played in *Hollywood Canteen*. Speaking of movie stars, I'd like to thank Miss Betty Grable for dropping in tonight. *(S.M. nods to cut-out on stage spotlighted briefly.)* She sustained a lot of soldiers with that pin-up pose of hers.

SCENE ONE:

REMEMBER PEARL HARBOR

(Music Cue: Bring up tape recording of "Remember Pearl Harbor." As it fades, S.M. continues narrative.)

S.M.: The war began in the fall of 1939 when Germany attacked Poland. Our nation remained divided. Some people favored intervention, and others believed we should remain neutral But reality prevailed. While the United States argued, France fell, and England endured the Blitz. We finally began to draft men into the Army in the fall of 1940, but a lot of people thought that we would never go to war. One East Texas man who got caught in that draft told me that he went AWOL in December so that he could come home for trapping season. The war seemed far away, but within a year, things had changed dramatically. Japan made the decision for us on December 7, 1941, with their attack on Pearl Harbor in the Hawaiian Islands. Do you remember where you were when you heard the news?

(S.M. turns on radio and FDR's speech to Congress is played on tape.)

S.M.: Hazel Shelton was a young girl in Nacogdoches in 1941: she has a vivid memory of that day.

HAZEL SHELTON: I was fourteen years old when World War II began—a sophomore at Nacogdoches High School. I remember coming out of the picture show that Sunday afternoon in December and hearing about the Japanese attack. An extra edition of *The Daily Sentinel* was already on the streets. The next day at school we listened to President Roosevelt's speech and the school band played "The Star-Spangled Banner." There wasn't a dry eye in the whole place.

S.M.: Howard White, A young man from Nacogdoches County, also remembers that day quite well. He was there!

HOWARD WHITE: After growing up as a sharecropper's son here in Nacogdoches County, I wanted to see the world. So, I joined the Navy in 1940 and served on several ships in the Pacific. I was serving on the *USS Raleigh* at Pearl Harbor on December 7. I remember going to my battle station in an anti-aircraft gun crew, but after a big explosion, I don't remember very much else. I got a concussion and abut the next thing I remember is waking up on a hospital ship headed for the U.S. I must have been the first casualty from Nacogdoches County in World War II. *(As White speaks, slides of Pearl Harbor are being shown.)*

SCENE TWO:

GOING TO WAR

S.M.: It wasn't long before thousands of East Texans were in uniform. Some could hardly wait to join up, while others waited for the mail to bring their "greetings." Regardless of how they entered the service, these East Texans were soon on their way to training camps all over the country. Listen as a few tell us about those early days of the war.

(Stage direction: Speaker is wearing khaki shirt and campaign cap to suggest he's in the army. He speaks in a strong forthright style—showing confidence.)

TERRY BONNER: Well, my name is Terry Bonner, and I'd joined the National Guard when I was still a kid in high school. When the 36th Division got called up in 1940, we were sent out to help build Camp Bowie at Brownwood. Somewhere along the way, I got sent to Fort Sill up in Oklahoma, where I finished high school. Growing up here in Marshall, I had a paper route, and I worked at the theater taking up tickets. I made about seven and a half a week, and that was pretty good in the Depression because times were hard. When that war came along over in Europe, I knew I was going to be in it. Somehow, I ended up in the Regular Army where I became part of the First Infantry Division—the Big Red One. This was the Regular Army, and we were among the first to leave for overseas. We crossed on the *Queen Mary*, and that was some experience. Well, after landing in Scotland, we ended up southwest of London where we continued to train for whatever the future held. As it turned out, it held a lot for me, because I was in on several invasions I'll tell you about those later.

PRICE RAMSEY: My name is Price Ramsey. I was a student at SFA when the war began. Some of my friends and I decided to join up right away. If you joined before the end of the term, you got your grades for that term. After training in the Navy, I went on a cruiser in the Pacific and served there for the entire war. I never got off that ship for a whole year—I mean I never touched land!

(Stage direction: Actor, as he speaks, takes off cardigan type sweater. He is wearing a blue shirt beneath and puts on a sailor cap.)

JACK LEACH: My name is Jack Leach. I joined the Marines in 1943 as soon as I graduated from high school. I already had two brothers in the service, and I didn't want to be left out. A friend and I hitchhiked down to Houston where I joined up. They later sent me to San Antonio where I was sworn in. I rode a train down there and that was the first time that I had ever been on a train. In fact, I soon experienced a lot of things for the first time. I had never been away from home—I thought Lufkin or Henderson was a long way off. When I got out to San Diego for boot camp, that was a whole new world. I had never seen a Coke dispenser—the type where you put in a nickel and a cup falls down, a little ice falls in it, and then the drink. When I stepped up to get my first payroll, I thought I was going to get a bunch of money, but they handed me only a few dollars. I was really let down, so I said, "Sir, there's been a mistake." The payroll officer later explained things to me. He told me that we had to pay for those things that I thought was free—things like toothpaste and a toothbrush and haircuts and laundry. Well, when he got through, I said, "Sir, I guess I'm lucky to have anything left."

GEORGE WEST: I'm George West from Panola County. Times were hard here before the war, and I worked at a variety of jobs. When we got into the war, several of my friends and I went over to Barksdale Field in Shreveport to join the Army Air Corps. A couple of us were put into the Aviation Cadets where we were going to learn to fly. They sent us to several bases and indoctrinated us and eventually began to teach us to fly. I remember the first time I got in an airplane—why, the only thing that I had ever flown before was a kite. And I thought to myself, "What in the hell have I got into here?". . .Within a year's time, I was flying missions over Germany.

S.M.: It seemed like everyone was going somewhere. In addition to the men and women who went off to war, an exodus occurred as workers left East Texas to take jobs in airplane plants and shipyards located here in Texas. A lot of people went up to the Dallas-Fort Worth area, while others went to shipyards in Beaumont and Orange. I remember talking to the Evans brothers from over around Hemphill. Both went down to the coast to build ships. Jodie started at the Consolidated Steel Shipyard at Orange in 1942 before moving to an oil refinery the next year. His brother John built Liberty Ships for Bethlehem Steel in Beaumont. Both had a lot of stories about the changes they experienced.

(Stage direction: As the following people talk, slides of industrial plants should be shown—pictures of naval ships and that type of thing.)

JODIE EVANS: I moved off to Orange because that was where the work was, but I didn't like living down there. We had to live in one of them public housing project things where the apartments were all squeezed up together—there was just a thin wall between you and your neighbors. There was no place for the kids to play except in the street. It was no place to raise kids.

(Stage directions: At this point two young boys—one about ten, the other seven or eight years old—enter the stage from opposite sides. They are dressed in rag-tag military uniform, perhaps a helmet and are carrying toy rifles or pistols. They pantomime war, aiming at one another, shooting, making "bang" noises. They slowly move toward a focal point on stage. Finally, one gives the death cry and falls to the floor. The other approaches. The boy on floor gets up.)

FIRST BOY: I'm tired of playing war, Billy. Why do I always have to be the Jap? Let's play cowboys.

SECOND BOY: Aw, come on, Jimmy. Even Gene Autry is making war movies. Didn't you hear President Roosevelt on the radio last night? He said we've all got to support this war effort. Playing war is the least we can do. My uncle fights in the real war, and I want to be like him.

FIRST BOY: *(He shrugs, shuffles his feet and then says:)* Hey, are you going over to Henderson to see that little Jap submarine they captured at Pearl Harbor? All you have to do is buy a war stamp, and they'll let you get up and look in it.

SECOND BOY: Sure! I'll ask my mom to take us over there—if she's got enough gas to get there and back. *(Both boys begin to walk off arm in arm.)* Let's play war some more. This time you can be a German.

JOHN EVANS: I'm Jodie's brother, John. I worked as a ship fitter for Bethlehem Steel. We built Liberty ships, the kind that hauled all that stuff overseas. I had taken my physical for the military but failed it because I had a scar on my lung. That didn't keep me from working though. You could work as much as you wanted to—there was plenty of overtime. I eventually made a dollar and twenty-five cents an hour and that was good pay. Why, I remember picking cotton for twenty-five cents a hundred pounds during harder times. I worked with some of the first women that came into the plan and I remember *(he chuckles)* that some of them hadn't had much experience in that type of work. One woman accidentally hit me on the knee with a sledge hammer. By the end of the war, a large proportion of workers in that plant were women.

S.M.: Women entered the work force in record numbers during World War II. "Rosie the Riveter" played a big role in defense plants all over the country. Of course, they didn't all work as riveters—some of them used sledge hammers, while others did tedious electronic work that required a steady hand. A good many worked in the foundries over in Lufkin, making gun carriages and other artillery parts. One young woman from Shelby County went off to defense school in Dallas before going to work for Consolidated Aircraft in Ft. Worth. She had a lot of memories.

(Show slides of working women.)

MOLLY UPTON: I'm Molly Upton. I grew up in Shelby County and went to college a little bit before the war started. I wanted to do my part, so I went up to Dallas and attended a government school to teach skills needed in defense work. I remember that it was in a big Pontiac Garage there, and it lasted about six weeks. I learned how to bend metal. Later, I got a job in Fort Worth at Consolidated Aircraft—helping to build B-24 bombers. They had a huge building over there. It must have been about a mile long. People had to ride bicycles up and down the line. I worked the swing shift from four p.m. to midnight. That meant that you couldn't go to any of those dance halls. My starting pay was eight-two cents an hour, and within a year's time I was making more than a dollar an hour. I didn't like the work and some of the people that you had to work with. I remember once that I got stuck with an old drunk and he kept making mistakes. I never did tell on him, but somebody did because he wasn't there very long. I eventually left to marry an airman that I had met, and we moved around quite a bit for the rest of the year.

(Perhaps song: "Rosie the Riveter" or something similar)

S.M.: Defense plans played a key role in the war effort, but someone had to build the military bases and training facilities scattered around this part of the country. I remember talking to one road contractor who worked on several of those projects.

B. H. MALLOY: I'm B. H. Malloy. I was a road contractor before the war, but everyone went into defense work once the war started. I helped to build some of the parking lots at those airplane plants up in the Dallas area and I even worked on Camp Fannin in Tyler. You were almost forced to do defense work whether you wanted to or not. They worked on a priority system and the only way to get any materials or any gasoline was to do defense work. Of course, I wanted to do my part, too. Boy, did we ever work hard; sometimes we worked around the clock, I guess you could say—time was of the essence. You could make good money, but you had to be a good contractor to do it. I went as far as Oklahoma to do some of my work—worked on a Naval Ordnance Plant up there near McAlester. I worked through the Army Engineers Office in Denison. They did a good job planning all those projects.

SCENE THREE

WOMEN IN WAR

S.M.: One military installation that didn't require much construction was right here in Nacogdoches. Like hundreds of other schools across the nation, Stephen F. Austin State Teachers College faced a bleak future during the war years. With most of the young men off in the service, the school's enrollment dropped off dramatically. At one point, it fell to about three hundred. Thanks to the hard work of President Paul Boynton and others, however, SFA found a way to keep going. Dr. Boynton arranged for a Women's Army Corps School to be set up at SFA for the purpose of training WACs in Army administration. Although it operated only a year in 1943-44, this facility trained several thousand women in Army office procedures. Each class of WACs remained on campus for six to eight weeks. Ironically, one of the first WAC officers to arrive at SFA was a native of Marshall, Texas—Gertrude Beasley.

(Stage direction: during this speech, slides of WAC scenes at SFA should be shown.)

GERTRUDE BEASLEY: The Army Administration School in Nacogdoches was my first real assignment after graduating from Officers Candidate School in Des Moines, Iowa. I thought it was my patriotic duty to join the Women's Army Corps during World War II. Of the nineteen grandchildren in my family, fifteen were girls, so we didn't send many men off to the war. My father didn't like the idea of my joining the Army, but my mother encouraged me. I was surprised when the WACs sent me to Nacogdoches, which was only eight miles from my hometown of Marshall. Our job here was to teach Army office procedures. I personally taught courses on finance and filing. There were thirty or forty to a class, and we went to school five and a half days a week. Some of the faculty members were male officers—the rest were women officers. The recruits came from all over America and from every walk of life. Most of them had joined the Army for patriotic reasons, and they resented being called "those WACs." They were just trying to do their duty. My assignment in Nacogdoches was really quite pleasant. I lived in a beautiful house just across the street from the campus. We were invited to various social events in town, and really stayed quite busy. *(Pauses)* Being in the WACs changed my life. I grew up.

I became a more tolerant person, and I learned many important lessons. I learned . . . *(thinks for a second and then answers with humor)* that there was life beyond Marshall, Texas.

HANNAH AARONSON: My name is Hannah Aaronson. To a nice Jewish girl from New York City, Nacogdoches, Texas, was quite different. We arrived by train, and then marched through the streets out to the college, where we were housed in some of the dormitories. There weren't many students around, especially male students, because most of them had gone off to the war. The facilities on this beautiful campus were wonderful. When we weren't in classes, we were allowed to act like college students. We could play games, lie around in the sun, or go downtown to the movie. One Saturday afternoon, four of us "Yankees" had gone to see the "western" movie *Stagecoach*. It was astonishing for us to sit in this movie house with all of these Texas people in western attire who were shouting and talking to the people in the movie. At one point when it got romantic, someone yelled out, "Hug her, kiss her." There was more action in the audience than on the screen! It struck us as very funny. For the most part, the citizens of Nacogdoches were loving and concerned. They accepted us and even invited us into their homes. I seldom passed anyone on the sidewalk who didn't speak to me. The town's people even set up a kind of USO club for us down on the square.

(Stage direction: At this point action shifts to a USO club set: a couple of tables with chair, a small dance floor, juke box if available. A small crowd gathers, including several WACs in khaki uniforms, plus a few high school age girls and one boy. Dance music comes up. Two high school girls are jitter-bugging together. Boy breaks in. Other girl pouts. A WAC is seated at a table by herself. She begins to talk about being in Nacogdoches—offers commentary contrary to other WAC's view. This is comic relief.)

UNHAPPY WAC: What am I doing down here in Texas? I was closer to the war when I was in New York City than I am in Nacogdoches, Texas. These people are something else. The food is terrible—it's all fried, and they eat too much cornbread. The weather is so hot and muggy you can't breathe. And the people are too friendly. Why you can't even walk down the street without everyone speaking to you. What's this world coming to? I miss New York!

(Scene livens up as music returns and dancers are active. At this point a trio of WACs gathers and sings maybe something like "Don't Sit Under the Apple Tree."

As song concludes lights come down on activity scene and return to WAC Aaronson who picks up her speech.)

AARONSON: During the short while I was here, I remember attending a graduation ceremony at the college. It was one of the most poignant things I have ever seen. Here we were in the middle of a war. There were virtually no male students, but life went on. We watched the small number of graduates, mostly girls, walking in their caps and gowns, along with their professors. It just struck me as an especially touching scene.

GERDA SPEAR: My name is Gerda Spear. My husband and I operated a clothing store here in Nacogdoches, and I came to know many of the WACs. So many of them were from back east, and they were not accustomed to our ways, but they became climatized pretty soon. And they liked it down here. They would come into the store. Well, you know how they feed Army people—pretty much on starches and fried foods. And they would come in and ask for a size 8, and I would sort of size them up and put a size 10 or 12 on them, and these clothes would fit them. And they would look at the size, and they would say, "Well, this fits, but this is a 12." And I would say, "Well, they make them sort of small." and they would say, "Gee, did I gain weight in the Army!" This was a typical response. We became friendly with lots of these girls, and we took them into our homes and our hearts. I can remember sometimes I would have fifteen or twenty girls over at my house for lunch on weekends. For a long time, I continued to correspond with several of these WACs. By and large, they were friendly. We enjoyed their friendship.

S.M.: The WACSs meant a lot to SFA and Nacogdoches. In fact, Dr. Boynton is still hailed as the Savior of SFA for having the foresight to bring them here. The sight of uniforms around town served as a reminder of what the war was all about. Not everyone was happy about the presence of so many females, however. SFA's basketball coach wondered why his school had to get women when other Texas colleges got men who could play basketball! And local high school girls found the added competition a little irksome in view of the shortage of boys. Some local housewives also were upset about the presence of so many extra females. In fact, one woman told me that if they hadn't got those WACs out of here, there was going to be a war in Nacogdoches.

(Play a portion of "Pistol Pack'n Mama" by Bing Crosby and the Andrews Sisters at this point.)

S.M.: Whether at home or abroad, the war went on. For some it proved adventurous—a time of new beginnings and fresh surroundings. For others, the war brought disruption and separation. Many turned inward for the strength to carry on, confident that a stronger force would see them through. A popular song by Irving Berlin seemed to sum it up:

(Song: "God Bless America")

INTERMISSION

ACT II

SCENE ONE

STAY-AT-HOMES

(Stage direction: Singers will perform a few WWII-era songs live as Act II begins.)

(Music cue: Music comes down and S.M. begins to talk about the experiences of those on the home front.)

S.M.: Despite the fact that fifteen million or so Americans served in the military—many of them overseas—the great majority of the population stayed at home during World War II. Aside from those who went off to work in defense plants or other war-related jobs, most East Texas continued their day-to-day existence. They were the glue that held the place together, and while most carried their own personal burdens because of the war, they often showed great courage. I suppose you could call it the East Texas version of the British "Stiff Upper Lip." I've talked with a number of those people, and their stories are wonderful, heart-warming accounts of a people who refused to let the war get them down. Listen to a few of them.

(Stage Direction: At this point the S.M. will turn on his tape recorder and a few taped excerpts will be played on the sound system.)

MABEL CLIFTON: My name is Mabel Clifton. My husband was drafted before the war began. He was sent to Ft. Benning, Georgia, and I followed him down there with two kids. It was hard to find a place to live around Ft. Benning. We ended up living in a three-room milk cooler located on a farm near there—that's just how hard it was to find a place to live. We had rats so big that we would shoot them with BB guns. We had gone to the movie on that Sunday when the war began. Now my grandmother and mother were quite religious, and they had always taught me you shouldn't go to the movie on Sunday. When we came out and I heard about that war, I thought I had caused it! But my husband quickly convinced me that it wasn't my fault. *(She chuckles)* After he went overseas, I returned to my hometown of Alto, Texas. By now, we had a young son in addition to my two young daughters. I was able to live in my mother's house and we got along okay. A group of us "War Widows" would meet every morning at the Post Office to check on our mail and see if we had any news. Then we would go down the street to Boyd's Drug Store where we would sit and drink coffee and Cokes and talk about our problems.

(Stage direction: scene shifts to Boyd's Drug Store in Alto, Texas. There will be a table with several women sitting around. As scene opens, they are talking and laughing. One woman wears a white apron—Mrs. Boyd. She serves Cokes. As Mabel Clifton enters, others greet her.)

MRS. BOYD: 'Morning, Mabel. Did you get any news today?

MABEL CLIFTON: *(Mabel sits down at table while talking.)* No letter today, but I got two yesterday. It's the same old stuff—no news. Those censors won't let them tell anything. Boy, I'll be glad when this war is over!

SECOND WOMAN: Mrs. Boyd, I need to fix up a package for my husband. He needs some soap and razor blades, and put in a few of those peanut patties, please. He says he's tired of all those chocolate bars they get.

MABEL C.: Does anyone have any extra sugar stamps? I need to bake a birthday cake for my son. This rationing sure does cramp my style.

THIRD WOMAN: I've got a few stamps you can have. Remember how I was wanting a shoe stamp last week? My daughter needed a new pair of shoes for her piano recital. Poor little thing—her toes were sticking out. Well, I went up to the rationing board—took her along to show them how bad she needed shoes. 'Course, I took the worst pair and showed them. I got the stamp, though, but now I can't find a pair of shoes anywhere. Guess I'll have to go over to Nacogdoches if I've got enough gas to get there.

MABEL C.: *(Laughing)* Well, here we are griping about shortages again, while our husbands are off fighting for us. What a war!

(Lights fade on drug store scene and scene returns to Mabel.)

MABEL C.: All we could do was just wait. I believe the war brought us all together. Sure, there was a lot of greed and a lot of those "4-F's" tried to take advantage of us "War Widows." And a few of them went along, but generally people pulled together. I always felt like my husband was off doing a job and what I had to do was to keep the home together. And I think that at least 90% of the people felt that way.

LEO BLACK: Well, I was one of those "4-F's," but I didn't want to be a slacker. I tried to do my part to help people during the war. I ran a filling station up in Tyler. I was examined several times for the draft, but I kept failing that exam because I had had some serious sickness earlier in life. But anyway, I worked hard in that filling station. We opened at six a.m. and I stayed open until ten o'clock at night. I thought it was my duty to help those women whose husbands were gone to keep their cars running, and I tried to do what I could to help people. Gas was rationed, of course, and you could only get a few gallons a week. And tires--"you just couldn't get any tires."

S.M: A lot of people found themselves doing things they had never done before. Some were involved in volunteer work, such as serving on draft and rationing boards. Others, especially women, joined Red Cross knitting circles. One woman even took a Red Cross nursing course just, so she could help other people. I talked with two women who served as aircraft spotters, one in rural Nacogdoches County and the other in Center.

(Actor designated aircraft spotter offers comment.)

AIRCRAFT SPOTTER: In addition to teaching school and driving a school bus, I "joined the Air Force." We watched at night for airplanes up in the Garrison area. We called in every plane that went over—

gave the directions and time so that someone could keep track of them. I don't think we missed a single one. See my arm band? *(She puts on air spotter arm band.)*

S.M.: Others were not so dramatic, but they also served the war effort.

KATIE WIGGINS: I'm Katie Wiggins. I lived on a farm up near Appleby during World War II. My husband failed his physical because he had back trouble and asthma, so he ended up going down to Orange to work in the defense plants. The main thing that I remember about World War II is being quite lonely. I had two young daughters at the time, and I tried to keep our farm going. I really didn't do much. I milked five or six cows every day, helped grind up feed for the cattle, and even hauled cotton to the gin—and, of course, I took care of my daughters. I did the best I could with the help of good neighbors, but I got awfully lonesome. I remember crying a lot.

(Song—"No Love, No Nothing.... I'm Lonesome...")

WIGGINS: My father and my sister would ride the train down from Garrison to visit with me, and my husband would come home on weekends when he could. But we just stayed here and tried to keep things going. You asked me what impact that war had on East Texas? Well, I'll tell you, I think that our young men found out a lot more about the world, and I think that they learned that they could branch out and do other things instead of staying poor on the farm.

ALBERT SUMMERVILLE: I'm Albert Summerville. I ran a typewriter and business machine place in Lufkin during World War II. I was over thirty years of age when the war began, and because I had been servicing some federal programs, I got a deferment. When the WAC school came to SFA, I got the contract to take care of their business machines, and I also serviced an Army program over at Sam Houston State Teachers College where they were training clerks. Didn't make a lot of money during the war, but I sure worked a lot of sixteen-hour days. The main thing that I learned from the war was how to deal with people. Later on, that helped me a lot in my business career. I do remember one humorous incident when I was servicing typewriters over at the prisoner of war camp near Huntsville—close to the Trinity River. They always assigned one of the German prisoners to help me. It was as kind of confusing because they usually had to work through an interpreter, and if you've never tried to give instructions about typewriter repair through an interpreter, you don't know how confusing things can get. But I had this young German man named Walter, who was a good boy, and he kept asking me if I would take him home with me and let him work in my shop in Lufkin. He saw the other prisoners going out to work in the timber industry and that type of thing and he wondered why he couldn't go to Lufkin and work in my shop. Well, I tried to explain to him that I didn't have any way to take care of him and we just couldn't do that. But he made me pretty nervous. I remember that every time I left that camp, once I got off the base, I would stop and look all in my car and look in the trunk because I was afraid that Walter would try to hide out and go home with me . . . I wonder whatever happened to Walter.

S.M.: Mr. Summerville's experience with German POWs was not uncommon because several thousand prisoners were scattered throughout the area in different camps. Many of them worked in agriculture or in the forest industry—mainly cutting wood for local lumber companies and Southland Paper Company over in Lufkin. Camps were located in both Nacogdoches and Angelina Counties, and it was not uncommon to see truckloads of prisoners. Most of them were hard workers who gave little though in escaping. Getting captured was the best thing that ever happened to them but being thousands of miles from home during a war was a traumatic experience, as one woman recalled.

SUE BURNS: My name is Sue Burns, and I remember one especially touching incident concerning those prisoners of war. I was a high school student during the war, and I played in a little musical ensemble that my mother directed. One Christmas we went out to the local POW Camp to entertain the American soldiers who served as guards. We were going to put on a little musical program in the afternoon. At the end of the program the Jr. High Choir sang "Silent Night." The program was being held in the mess hall out there and there were some German POWs who were cleaning up. As the choir sang that song, a lot of those boys would get tears in their eyes and sing along in German. The Camp Commander later asked us if we would come back that evening and put on a program for the POWs. And we did. It was quite touching.

(As she talks the tape-recorded rendition of "Silent Night" being sun in German plays in the background.)

(As choir completes "Silent Night," S.M. comments on a POW he interviewed.)

S.M.: I had an opportunity to talk with a former German prisoner a while back. He had come back to Chireno, Texas, where he had been imprisoned in a work camp during the war. The town turned out for what amounted to a party, complete with speeches and refreshments. He later told me that he had kept in touch by letter with several of the local people after the war. Obviously moved by such a reception, he said that he never expected to be treated in such a friendly manner. Such are the vagaries of war.

Many of the POWs who worked in this area came from a larger contingent up at Camp Fannin near Tyler. The camp was named for the legendary Col. James Fannin of Texas history fame. It was an Infantry Replacement Center. More than a quarter of a million men underwent training there. Most went overseas upon completion of the sixteen-week program because replacements were vital from 1943 until the later days of the war. Tyler was a sleepy East Texas city when the camp was built in 1943, but things soon changed. A lot of civilians found work at this larger military installation. One of them was Lena Hammond who worked in the Headquarters building.

LENA HAMMOND: I went to work at Camp Fannin before the base was opened. This was in 1943, and the camp was just being built. At times, I was embarrassed because I just didn't have very much to do. But we got busier as the base opened. I worked in the Base Commander's Office. The actual training of the men took place up on the "hill," and we didn't know very much about that. They had their own cadre, but we had to handle all the housekeeping functions and it was a tremendous job. Later the base housed a number of German prisoners of war. I shall never forget the first time that I saw those men. They came marching through our part of the camp with shovels and rakes on their shoulders—marching four abreast and singing their marching songs. It was scary to me. They worked in our flower beds, and I was always a little uneasy. The Officers use to kid us and say they would protect us. *(Pauses after a bit)* I didn't know many of the men who were there for training, but I was aware that these men would soon be in battle because we were a replacement center. My own husband was overseas. Every day I prayed for him and the men of Camp Fannin—men who were thinking about their own wives and sweethearts—planning for a future that they might never have. Thousands of them would be wounded or killed.

NORMAN COOPER: My name is Norman Cooper, and I was one of those trainees at Camp Fannin. I endured several months of the Texas heat in the summer of 1943. I don't know if the weather records would bear this out, but I don't think it rained the entire summer. And all of us had prickly heat. We had to make these long, forced marches on the back roads around the camp. And we would pass through these little communities with our full field packs, overcoats and even wearing gas masks. It was torturous. Some of those old "Nesters" would be sitting on the porches of grocery stores and filling stations, and they would shout out encouragement to us. "Go get 'em, boys." Some of them had probably been in the first World War. I also recall that we were very well-received by the people of Tyler—at least, when I went into town to church the people were always friendly to me. One family invited me home to Sunday dinner, and I met the girl who later turned out to be my wife.

JOHNNY COOKE: I'm Johnny Cooke from Marshall, Texas, and I also did my basic training over there at Camp Fannin. I was born out near Karnack in 1917. After attending country schools, I graduated from Marshall High School in 1935—sometimes I rode a horse to school. That was during the Depression, and jobs were hard to find. I finally ended up working as a local experience man for the Civilian Conservation Corps camp near Marshall. I later attended SFA down in Nacogdoches for a term or so in 1938. Later, when the war came along, I was finally inducted into the Army at Camp Wolters, but by a stroke of luck they sent me back to Camp Fannin for my training. In the meanwhile, I got married, and even though I wasn't far from home, I missed my wife bad. That training was hard, but I was tough. I could work from daylight to dark. As we were leaving Camp Fannin, I remember one of the sergeants telling us, "Boys, the government has spent about ten thousand dollars training each of you—now, don't you go very there and get your ass shot off." I left East Texas in early 1944 and finally ended up in the Pacific where I saw action in the Philippines and finally in Okinawa. I joined an infantry unit as a replacement. My job was carrying ammunition to the front. The sergeant was right; they were shooting at us. I expected to be in on the invasion of Japan, but the war ended, I came back to Marshall and did conservation work until I retired in the mid-1970's.

S.M.: Most of the trainees were young men in their late teens and early twenties. Some older men in their thirties found the intense physical training quite difficult, as this excerpt from a letter indicates. *(S.M. reads from letter.)*

"They are pouring it on guys, with these long marches and it's hard on us old men; we just barely keep up with these young boys. Did you hear what General MacArthur said about Camp Fannin boys? He said not to send him anymore because they were worn out when they got there."

Besides such individual acts of patriotism, entire groups joined in worthwhile projects aimed at easing the pain of war. Many East Texas towns had Red Cross groups that knitted and prepared bandages. In Marshall, a group of Red Cross women met and served refreshments to troop trains headed who knows where. Listen as Ellen Rogers—one of those volunteers—tells how she spent many a day at the Marshall depot handing out cookies and other snacks to travelling GI's.

ELLEN ROGERS: Marshall was a big railroad center during World War II. The Texas and Pacific Railroad had a large shop installation here. In fact, my husband worked there as an electrician. A lot of troop trains passed through here, just filled with lonesome soldiers headed all over the country. Thanks to Mrs. Fannie Nichols, the local Red Cross got up a good service program to provide little snacks for the troops. This was a pretty large program that involved, oh, around fifty or sixty women, I suppose. We were well organized. Some days we might get three or four troop trains through Marshall, so we needed volunteers down there most of the day. We had two shifts: one worked from eight to noon and the other from noon until 5 p.m. It seems like there was always someone at the station. The Camp Fire girls also helped us hand out refreshments. Those boys were so sweet. We had one old white-haired lady who was a volunteer, and they'd gather around her and call her "Grandma." Sometimes tears would run down their faces. They were so appreciative. When a train came in, we'd just circulate up and down the platform with our little baskets of food. The trains would be here for only a short while, but I believe we cheered up a lot of those soldiers. They didn't know where they were going, and I often thought of how many might not come back. It made you feel so good to know that you were doing something for them. Most of those volunteers are gone now—I may be the last one alive.

ROY LONG: My name is Roy Long, and I happened to be on one of those troop trains that passed through Marshall. I remember it just like it was yesterday when the ladies met us at the train with the cookies and the punch. They went from window to window serving us. We were headed for Camp Blanding in Florida, and Marshall was the only place that offered such hospitality. I eventually served in a hospital unit in the Pacific—out in the middle of a jungle. Little did I know that years later I would end up moving to Marshall where I've been in business since the 1950's. It was just a coincidence that I came here, but I must have liked those cookies.

S.M.: Staying in touch by letter was important during the war. Mail call proved to be the vital link that tied the home front to the training camps and battle zones. Numerous persons have told me that they wrote their loved ones every day. Letters from overseas were less frequent, but plenty of V-mail moved across the oceans. One of the champion letter writers of the war was Mattie Jones from right here in Nacogdoches County.

MATTIE DAVIS: My husband and I had twelve nephews in the service during World War II—plus our son and a son-in-law. In addition, I wrote to several of the boys from our community. I was writing letters all the time.

(Stage direction: As Mrs. Davis concludes comments, S.M. picks up the topic and introduces letter-writing scene. This scene will portray the experiences of Edward Gage, a Nacogdoches boy who joined the Marines and went off to the war. This scene portrays his experiences through portions of letters written home. S.M. will comment at appropriate places, while actor recites from letters. Actor is prominently portrayed and lighted elsewhere on stage. He begins by talking about his early training. He is wearing a khaki uniform. As he gets to battle zone, he puts on a fatigue top and cap and sits on a tree stump while writing. He speaks as he writes, with S.M. offering explanatory remarks.)

S.M.: Perhaps nothing is so personal as the thoughts and feelings that one puts down on paper and sends to someone else. Edward Gage was a young Nacogdoches high school graduate who joined the Marine Corps in late 1942. Over the next three years or so, he carried on a long correspondence with his parents, which eventually resulted in several hundred letters. He shared some of those with me in an effort to provide a case study of his small role in the war. Within that brief three years, he went from Nacogdoches to training sites here in the United States and finally shipped out to the Pacific, where he underwent further training in Hawaii before joining the battle at Leyte in the Philippine Islands. Gage joined the Marines while he was a student at Stephen F. Austin State Teachers College. He was soon on his way to the V-12 Officers' Training Program at Louisiana Tech College at Ruston, Louisiana. But color-blindness changed his plans, however, and soon he was in the regular Marines, undergoing boot camp at San Diego, California.

ED GAGE: *(He gives date of each letter as he begins.)* "14 October 1943. My first week in boot camp has been one of the toughest I ever spent. From 5:30 a.m. to 10 at night, we're double-timed through drills, meals, washing ourselves and our clothing, cleaning our barracks, and everything else we do. All the while our drill instructors are breathing fire and brimstone down our necks . . ."

S.M.: Upon completing boot camp, Gage began his journey to war. He was assigned to the Field Artillery, where his color blindness proved to be an advantage. It enabled him to see through camouflage and to detect targets that those with normal vision could not see.

His boat trip from California to Hawaii was a moving experience.

ED GAGE: "1 February 1944. I made the trip mostly by rail. That is, I suffered terrible sea-sickness most of the time. You feel like you are going to die, but you know you won't and that makes it all the worse."

S.M.: While undergoing further training in Hawaii, Gage had a pleasant experience before entering the horrors of battle.

ED GAGE: "19 July 1944. We really had a surprise recently. Bob Hope, Frances Langford, Jerry Colonna, and others appeared in person for a show at our camp. It was great."

S.M.: After completing training in August of 1944, Gage and his battalion boarded several ships bound for combat. They spent more than a month at sea in one of the largest convoys ever assembled in the Pacific. He was going to Leyte Island in the Philippines.

ED GAGE: "20 October 1944. I'm on Leyte in the Philippine Islands and thus far have been a shade busy. However, I'm okay, though, and have been very fortunate. Thank God."

S.M.: What his parents didn't know was that he had two near brushes with death while landing on Leyte. The first came while he was crawling down a landing net into a smaller boat. A Japanese suicide plane strafed the side of the ship and later crashed into a nearby vessel, killing numerous Americans. Once he got out of the landing boat, he went over his head in the water and almost drowned because of the weight of his equipment.

(Stage direction: At this point Gage has changed to fatigue equipment and is sitting on a stump pretending to be writing a letter.)

S.M.: He was soon in the thick of battle, and even though the artillery ordinarily fought behind the infantry, he experienced numerous clashes with Japanese patrols and considerable fighting. He especially remembered one incident where they fired their canons for what seemed like an eternity. As they moved up, Gage said the stench of decaying human flesh was so strong that he had to hold a wet cloth over his face. During his two months in battle on Leyte, Gage lost 48 pounds. He suffered fever and other assorted ailments.

ED GAGE: "9 November 1944. Our experiences in war make us more considerate of our buddies and others. We work and share alike. War also makes us appreciate life in general . . . It's amazing how wonderful the sunlight of the early morning is after an anxious night."

S.M.: War had its lighter side, however, as this letter reveals.

ED GAGE: "12 November 1944. We had one of those tropical storms the other night . . . The enlisted men's portable eight-hole toilet floated away on the torrent of the stream beside which we were camped. We were left in a bad way."

S.M.: But the big brass came to the rescue when they ordered the officers to share their toilet with the enlisted men. As Gage noted, "It was a case of instant democracy at work." Late in December of 1944, Gage wrote that at least he had left the Philippines. "It's been a trying experience under very adverse conditions," he said, "and although it could have been worse, we're all pretty well worn." He later participated in mop-up actions on Guam, where he made this observation about war:

ED GAGE: "1 April 1945. This is a grim game, the worst there is; and we have to be alert at all times. But if we allow fear to govern our alertness, we won't last two seconds."

S.M.: The end of the war in the summer of 1945 found Gage on Guam, awaiting the American invasion of Japan. A month or so later he was on a ship headed for the United States. Gage later told me that he was more fortunate than many others. He escaped physically, but he was marked in unseen ways that would last a lifetime. As he put it, he had been "purified in the crucible of war."

(Stage direction: lights down on Marine. Scene shifts.)

S.M.: As the war drug on, more and more young men found themselves entering the military. This was a traumatic experience for families and friends here at home. Hazel Shelton has some wonderful stories about those days.

HAZEL SHELTON: The war began to come home to us as our friends went off to be involved. The class of 1939 lost several boys. I remember being in the principal's office one day when word came that one of our former students had been killed. One of the teachers was in the office and she began to cry, and the principal, Mr. Chambers, just went back into his office and closed the door. Our little group tried to do nice things for the boys who had to leave. I remember when Oliver was drafted. We took up money and bought his girlfriend a ticket, so she could accompany him to Houston. Of course, her parents didn't know anything about this, but it was perfectly innocent. They were chaperoned the whole time. But when she got back the next day, her parents were quite unhappy, and she got grounded for a month. That seemed to me the most romantic event that occurred during the whole war.

S.M.: One of my more interesting interviews concerned an East Texas bus line that hauled a lot of people to and fro during those troubled years. Since gasoline was scarce, people rode the bus virtually everywhere. Airline Motor Coaches served most of East Texas then, especially the runs from Houston to Shreveport and from Tyler to Beaumont. Their headquarters was right here in Nacogdoches. Busses were probably the most common form of public transportation during the war. Many a homesick soldier found himself staring out the window of a bus. One poet captured the melancholy of it all when he noted:

"Oh, all the wars in Germany and Russia will not make them grieve like a Shell Station, and Lone Star Bar and the Hotel Davie Crocket."

He must have passed through Texas!

BETTY MCKENZIE: I'm Betty McKenzie, and I worked as a ticket agent for Airline. I'll tell you one thing—those busses were full. People stood in the aisles and sat on their suitcases. Service men got the first seats--that was company policy. A lot of busses came in about 1:30 in the morning, and since I lived across the street from the station I would sometimes go over and give the night crew a hand. It seemed like everyone was going somewhere.

(Stage direction: scene shifts to bus station in Nacogdoches. Pretty young woman behind ticket counter. A short line of customers—young woman, older woman, and young airman. Each has suitcase. Small talk ensues as patrons buy tickets. Lights up on ticket counter moved on stage.)

TICKET AGENT: Where are you going honey?

YOUNG WOMAN: I need a ticket to Mineral Wells. I'm going to see my husband. He's stationed at Camp Wolters. They're about to ship him out.

AGENT: I know how you feel—my brother's over at Fort Benning in Georgia. *(She sells ticket to woman who moves away.)*

OLDER WOMAN: Could I buy a ticket to Beaumont? My husband is working down at the shipyard.

AGENT: Sure, we've got an extra running tonight—it's due in here any minute. Is that one way or round trip?

WOMAN: One way. He's found us a little garage apartment down there. I hate to move, but we've been a part so long. *(She takes ticket, pays agent and moves on.)*

AGENT: How about you, corporal? Where are you going? *(Airman steps up to counter.)*

AIRMAN: Give me a one-way to Shreveport, please. I've got to get back to Barksdale Field quick. My leave's almost up. I' guess I'll be going overseas soon—I hope the war lasts until I can get there.

AGENT: Well, we'll do our best to get you to Shreveport, but you may have to sit in the aisle. Good luck.

(Lights down as "Sentimental Journey" comes up on sound system. Scene shifts back to S.M.)

SCENE TWO

FIGHTING THE WAR

S.M.: A lot of those bus rides were the first stage of a journey to the war zones. I've already pointed out that thousands of Texas served in the military during the war, and that a good many of those came from East Texas. They went all over the world, and some didn't come back. Most did, especially the ones that you're hearing from tonight. Many of them are still around somewhere in East Texas. In fact, you might be sitting next to one of them right now... When Bert Akin shipped out for the Philippines in the fall of 1941, he had little reason to believe that he would spend most of the war in a Japanese prisoner of war camp. We weren't even at war with Japan yet, but that soon changed.

BERT AKIN: I was in the Philippine Islands when the war began. My unit shipped out from Manila on Christmas Eve, 1941. We ended up on the Bataan Peninsula, where a lot of bad fighting took place. I was eventually captured, and we had to make that terrible Bataan Death March. A lot of people died. There wasn't much fear in my heart. I knew that I was in for a rough situation, but a man just gets to where he lives from minute to minute—you can't think of the worst. You only want to think of the best. I ended up in Japan working in a coal mine for the rest of the war, but I always believed that God guides a man's footsteps, and I believed that a man would make it regardless of where he was headed if it was the Lord's will.

S.M.: Mr. Akin's niece later told me that she was working with her father on a farm outside Nacogdoches when word of her uncle's capture arrived. "My father dropped to his knees and cried," she said. "He thought he would never see his brother again. But he did." For others, the war was a protracted experience that ranged from boredom to sheer fright. Here's what several of them had to say.

PRICE RAMSEY: *(Ramsey wears a sailor cap.)* I'm Ramsey. I've already told you that I left SFA and joined the Navy. I eventually ended up on the *USS Mobile*. We spent the entire war in the Pacific, and it seemed like I would never get off that ship. I went a whole year without ever touching land. We experienced Kamikaze attacks and typhoons, participated in sea battles and landings, and finally ended up in Japan. It sure was a long way from East Texas.

TERRY BONNER: It's Terry Bonner again. I promised I'd tell you about a few of my war experiences. Being among the first troops arriving in England, I had the privilege of being in several invasions. In 1942, we landed in Algeria during the invasion of North Africa. I was right in the middle of all that fighting which finally ended up with the defeat of Rommel's forces. I remember that one of our two officers in the Big Red One was General Teddy Roosevelt, Jr. Now, he was a real soldier. Later, in July of 1943, I got in on the invasion of Sicily. We made our landing about 2 a.m., and I can tell you that there was some bad fighting. I was scared all the time. The worst thing was moving back up to the front after you'd had a few days of rest. One time we marched fifty miles in seven hours and then spent forty-eight hours in constant combat. I really didn't think I'd ever come back from that war. My group later returned to England to train for the invasion across the English Channel into France. We were in the first wave of troops on June 6, 1944—D-Day. Omaha Beach was our destination, and that was some of the worst fighting I ever saw. We finally clawed our way up that beach and hung on. Later, after the break-through, we went to the outskirts of Paris and then moved on into Belgium just in time to participate in part of the Battle of the Bulge. When the war ended, I was in Czechoslovakia. I had walked my entire way across Europe. We didn't know what vehicles were. On the last day of the war in Europe, I was wounded and sent back to the U. S. Several months later, I was released from the hospital in San Antonio. The war was the greatest experience of my life. I had seen a lot of the world, won a few medals, and even met the famous war correspondent, Ernie Pyle. That was pretty good for a paper boy from Marshall, Texas.

NATHAN COLE: My name is Nathan Cole. Unlike Mr. Bonner, I did a lot of riding during World War II, because I was in a transportation unit. We hauled food and ammunition and other supplies all over parts of Europe. I was born near Chireno in 1922 and later attended E. J. Campbell High School in Nacogdoches. I left school after the tenth grade to join the Civilian Conservation Corps Camp located near Nacogdoches. This was known as a "colored" camp, and we did soil conservation work. But I got to work in the shop learning how to be a mechanic. That training came in handy later on. I was drafted into the Army in December of 1942. We knew we were going to be in that war back when I was in the CCC camp. I rode a bus out to Camp Wolters near Mineral Wells where we were inducted and then we did our training there for several months. Later, I had some more training over at Camp Swift near Bastrop. Then we were switched over to a quartermaster trucking outfit and shipped to Boston where we left for Europe early in 1943. It took our convoy about fourteen days to get to Liverpool, England. We immediately started to unload ships and deliver goods all over that part of England. Now, our unit was an all-black group, but we had white officers, although some of our noncommissioned officers were blacks. I made sergeant myself. I remember being bombed by German planes and having to jump into those ditches. We were hauling gasoline and we were afraid we were going to be blown up right there in England. About a month after the D-Day landing, we went to France ourselves, but the fighting had moved on into France by that time. Well, we hauled all kinds of stuff—ammunition, food, clothing. Finally, we ended up over there in Germany. We were hauling for Patton. So, when we got there, he was gone, and we had to find out where he was. I got pretty close to that war, and I want to tell you I was scared most of the time. But you get used to it. I remember being bombed and having the fragments fall on us while we hid in those ditches. It was scary. After the war ended in Europe, we went back to France and shipped out on the same ship that we had ridden over from Boston—the *U.S.S. Brazil*. We were headed for the Pacific to take part in the invasion of Japan. By the time we got to the Philippine Islands, the war had ended, and we finally came home. Yessir, I did a lot of traveling during that war, but I sure was glad to get home.

(*Song: Anchors Aweigh*)

JACK LEACH: (*Leach puts on a helmet as he begins to speak*) I told you about all those new experiences I had after joining the Marines. Well, I really had a new experience when I got to the Pacific—there were people shooting at me! We got in on the fighting at Okinawa, and it was pretty rough. I remember that I got hit by some shrapnel—it just kind of felt like a bee had stung me. But when I looked down and saw blood coming up out of my boot, I wondered if I was going to live to be twenty years old. That was on June 17, 1945—two days before my birthday.

S.M.: Jack was lucky. A lot of people weren't. United States battle deaths amounted to about 300,000. You saw a lot of those little blue-star banners hanging in the windows of families that had someone in the service. *(S.M. points to banner hanging on stage.)* When a person was killed, gold stars replaced the blue ones. Families lived in fear of receiving the dreaded telegram.

(Play tape of telegraph sound behind Sloan's speech.)

J. P. SLOAN: My name is J. P. Sloan. I was a railway agent at Leggett down near Livingston. In small stations like that, you also handled the Western Union Line. Many a day I sat there and listened to death messages going down the wire. "We regret to inform you . . ." it went something like that. I could just imagine the sorrow that accompanied those messages.

S.M.: We sometimes overlook the fact that the enemy suffered horribly in this war. Japan alone lost more than a million in battle deaths. George Hicks, an Angelina County man who joined the Army, remembered the slaughter that took place in the mop-up action in New Guinea.

GEORGE HICKS: I joined the Army as soon as I turned eighteen. I did my training at Camp Wolters near Mineral Wells. I was number 38498393. The main thing that I remember about that place was cactus, rocks, and horned toads. We ended up in New Guinea, where the Japanese were just about starved out. They even resorted to cannibalism. The story was that they ate the Privates first; then the Corporals and Sergeants gave up because they knew there were next on the menu. They sometimes made suicide charges, and we just mowed them down with our machine guns.

S.M.: We haven't said much about airplanes so far. Now, everyone knows that World War II was an air war, but don't try telling that to the infantry. Nevertheless, airplanes played a big role. A Marshall man—Joe Johnson—was among an elite group of about a thousand African Americans who learned to fly in World War II and served in the Air Force. Although he never got overseas, he played an important role in the Tuskegee air program.

JOE JOHNSON: I'm Joe Johnson, and I go way back in Marshall history. I was born on the campus of Wiley College where my father was a teacher. I later attended Wiley from 1936 'til I graduated in 1941. I was a football player in those early days, and they said I was one of the best pass catchers in this area. I weighed one hundred seventy pounds, and I was fast. The war came long about the time I got out of college, and it really affected my life. I had planned to be a teacher, but when that war started, I wanted to join the Air Force. I'd only seen one airplane close up and that had been several years before. Well, I went over to Barksdale field in Shreveport and told them that I wanted to learn how to fly. But most of the black fellows I saw over there seemed to be doing just regular menial work—cleaning up and that type of thing. But I knew that they were going to start a program that would allow African Americans to learn how to fly, and I intended to be part of it. After all kinds of tests and military training—I went into the military in early 1942—I was finally sent to Tuskegee, Alabama, where a pilots' program for African Americans was beginning. We went through all kinds of training—pre-flight, primary training—all that type of thing. I remember that the first plane I flew in was a PT-17—a bi-wing airplane made of canvas. Flying didn't scare me. In fact, I liked it. We had one interesting incident that happened during that period. One of my fellow students had to make a forced landing nearby and as he was getting out of the airplane, a group of little white kids ran up and asked, "Where's the pilot?" Many of the people in that program were from up north; they were all college graduates, and many of them had been star athletes. As we progressed through different stages of training, we finally got to fly those used by the Flying Tigers in China. I was eventually part of the 332nd Fighter Group. Unfortunately, I didn't get to go overseas with the rest of my friends. I remained at Tuskegee as an instructor, so I guess they thought I knew how to fly. Only about a third of the guys in each class finally graduated. In all, we had about nearly a thousand who graduated and got their wings, and about 450 went overseas, where many of them were involved in combat. In fact, three of my former roommates were killed flying out of Italy. After the war, I took training to be an aeronautical engineer, but I was unable to find a job in California. So, I went to work in the Post Office and stayed there for thirty-six years. I did spend about six or seven years working for Hughes Aircraft on satellite programs, so I guess you can say that I went all the way from bi-wing airplanes to satellites. Being in World War II was a turning point in my life. I never thought I'd learn how to fly. I'm still active in the Tuskegee Airmen's Group, but there's not many of us left now.

S.M.: Some of the most heroic stories concern those airmen who crawled into those planes day after day to bomb some distant target. Airplanes seemed to have personalities of their own, and many of them carried names right up there on the fuselage. One Carthage man who served as crew chief in England said he got to name several planes in his flight. One proudly carried the words, "Via Panola Express" in honor of his home county. Ted Ray, a former Jacksonville high school football player, christened his plane, "Texas Chubby, the J'ville Jolter." A picture of a long-haired Indian beauty was in honor of the Jacksonville Indians. It also had something to do with his wife, I believe. Another wife found herself portrayed on the nose of an airplane, and therein lies an East Texas story. Let's let Louise West tell it:

LOUISE WEST: Well, George and I had been married for five years when he left to join the Air Corps. He and several of his best friends from Carthage joined up over at Barksdale Field in Shreveport. He wound up flying a B-17 for the 8th Air Force out of England. I sent him a picture of myself in a pair of shorts—sort of bending over, you know. The next thing I knew he had someone draw that picture on his airplane, which he named the "West End." He even had it embroidered on the back of his flight jacket.

S. M.: Let's let George get in a word:

(Song: Air Force Songs—"Off We go . . .")

GEORGE WEST: It was a good airplane. We made twenty-eight missions over Europe and never had anyone killed or even wounded. But we did catch a lot of flak. It sounded like gravel thrown on a tin roof; every mission was a close call. Once we came back on two engines. They later scrapped the plane. I wasn't too scared until one of my Carthage friends went down in the English Channel. After that it was hard to get back into that plane, but I made ten more missions and came home. When the war ended, I was flying B-29s and getting ready to go to Japan.

S.M.: J. T. Hammill of Sabine County had a view from the other end of the airplane. He was a tail-gunner in a B-17. He flew thirty-five missions out of England, but his luck almost ran out on one of them.

J. T. HAMMILL: We were on a mission to Hamburg—we were hitting the oil refineries there. I had never seen so much flak before. You could almost get out and walk on the stuff. And we lost I don't know how may planes. I was scared. Anyway, we lost an engine and the pilot tells the co-pilot, "Feather number three—it's not doing us any good either." We're still over Germany. I called up the pilot: I says, "Are we going to ride this thing home or are you going to bail us out?" After a little while he said, "I'm going to take it home." And I said, "Well, I'm riding with you, then—take us home." We were struggling along and there came the North Sea. Boy, that water looked cold down there! Pretty soon the Captain said to the co-pilot, "You might as well feather number four. It's wind-milling too much." So, there we were with only one engine. The Captain figures that he could glide the thing to the English Coast. Just as we got to a little RAF base, the last engine died—we were about eight or ten feet off the ground, so he just bellied that sucker in. It tore up that B-17, but we all walked away. Like the old song said, I guess we were "coming in on a wing and a prayer."

(Sound direction: at this point bring up song, "Coming in on a Wing and a Prayer." Play a little and fade out as S.M. makes final speech.)

FINALE

THE WAR ENDS

S.M.: World War II was full of stories like that. Others didn't turn out so well. The military cemeteries scattered throughout Europe and the Pacific are proof of that. The war finally ended in the late summer of 1945, and millions of Americans headed home. Those who returned to East Texas found the same little towns and communities, but something was different. The area had changed. People had been places. As one woman noted, "every time we saw a pickup truck coming down the road, we'd say, 'there comes another one home from the shipyards.'" In fact, many of them have only recently begun to come home—back from the refineries and the chemical plants on the coast, back from the industrial and business complexes located elsewhere in the state. Many of the veterans themselves found that they had to seek work in those places. But there was work in a variety of ways.

(At this point S.M. picks up interview with Mr. Wingo from beginning of play. He goes over to carousel which has been returned to the scene--table, two chairs, Mr. Wingo is seated. S.M. walks over and continues interview.)

S.M.: Tell me, Mr. Wingo, after seeing all that destruction at Pearl Harbor, and then fighting the rest of the war, did you hate the Japanese?

FRED WINGO: Yeah, I suppose everyone hated the Japanese a little bit.

S.M.: By the way, what did you do after the war was over?

WINGO: Oh, I was in the car business most of the time *(at this point he chuckles and says)* I guess it's a little bit ironic, but right now I'm business manager for a Toyota agency!

(Lights fade on carousel and S.M. gets up and returns to his position where he concludes the play.)

S.M.: It took a while for Toyotas to get to East Texas, but this area was mightily changed by World War II. The old agricultural ways were transformed. Row crop farming virtually disappeared, but chickens and dairy cattle were just around the corner along with considerable industrialization. East Texas today is a far different place from what it was in the 1940's. Now some of this change would have occurred if the war had never happened. But it's hard to envision it happening so quickly without the impetus of that momentous event which is now fifty years in the past.

(Stage direction: by this time the readers have left the stage as the S.M. delivers his final speech in preparation for curtain calls.)

S.M.: Before we leave, I'd like to say several "thank yous": To the actors, who did a fine job; to Miss Grable, for gracing our stage; to you for coming; and finally, to the people of East Texas, who have shared their experiences—thanks for the memories.

(Music comes up with song "Thanks for the Memories." Curtain call.)

EAST TEXAS TALKS
A Radio Play in Two Acts

by
Bobby H. Johnson

NOTES

Technology has changed since this play was written in 2009. The director has permission to use modern technology. The interviews are at Stephen F. Austin State University in the East Texas Research Center, and they are being put on line. Music played a big part in the production of this play, however, this publication does not grant permission to use the music suggested. The music titles mentioned are suggestions, and others may be substituted or not used as appropriate.

Since this play is portraying a radio show, the director may use local musical talent, but keep to the style of the play.

In 1990, Sarah McMullan, director of Lamp-Lite Players, suggested Bob "do something" with his interviews, and this play is one example. Because of health problems, Bobby has not been involved in getting the plays ready for publication. It is my hope that community theatres, drama departments, and history classes will use these plays, sometimes as community service. Lamp-Lite Theatre, Nacogdoches, TX, has presented his plays as Reader's Theatre at Magnolia Court, an assisted living facility in Nacogdoches, and they were well-received. Even though the plays are about East Texas, the characters represent people and their lives everywhere.

Myrna Johnson, Bobby's left hand

2020

ABOUT THE PLAY

East Texas Talks is the culmination of something that started nearly 40 years ago. My first oral history project (on the East Texas Oil Boom) occurred during the summer of 1970. I was a relatively young assistant professor of history at Stephen F. Austin State University, and my subsequent efforts resulted in more than 500 interviews about the region. My relation to East Texas began in 1935 when I was born at Overton, right in the middle of the East Texas Oil Field. We lived at New London where my father worked for the Humble Oil & Refining Co. (now Exxon). He worked in the recovery of bodies following the New London school explosion of 1937, which resulted in the deaths of about 300 children and teachers. It was a haunting experience I attempted to portray in my last play, *A Texas Tragedy*, presented at the Lamp-Lite in 2005 and revised into a one-act play, which was entered in the district Interscholastic League competition by Huntington High School in 2008. It did not advance, but the cast did a wonderful job!

The characters you hear are the voices of East Texas: hard-working, honest people whose experiences unite us all in the common problems and joys of life regardless of where we faced them. The musicians strongly amplify their messages. Enjoy!

ABOUT THE AUTHOR

For those who might want to know more about me, I'm a native East Texan who later grew up in the Houston area. I always thought this completed my childhood years. I went to college in West Texas, a proud graduate of Abilene Christian College as it was then called. I majored in journalism, which is my first love because it taught me to tell stories. I briefly worked in the newspaper world for a few years, including a short stint in Little Rock, Arkansas, during the civil rights problems that community faced. I then went to the University of Oklahoma, where I studied journalism and American history. I earned both M.A. and Ph.D. degrees there. After that I came to SFA in 1966, and I've been here ever since. I rose to become a Regents Professor of History. It's been a blessing to talk to the people of East Texas over the years, and I hope I've left some impression on the region.

Bobby H. Johnson

February 2009

EAST TEXAS TALKS

CHARACTERS
Stage Manager (S.M.)
Centenarian
Teacher
    School Scene
Professor
Oil Field Hand
Preacher
    New London Scene
    Ab Allen
Patriot
    Drug Store Scene
    Tom Nader
Pragmatist
Papermaker
Farmer

Piano/Harmonica Interludes

Outsider
Insider
War Bride
Wright Family and Friends (Sacred Harp)
Gospelorians (Gospel Quaartet)
Organizer
Fur Man
Hippie
Undertaker
Teenager
Mollie and Mary
Modern Granny

Piano/Harmonica Interludes

NOTE: We will use a radio-show format, with actors portraying various East Texas characters and musicians presenting pertinent songs and tunes before a live audience. The setting will be a simple radio studio, complete with microphones and perhaps some sound effects. The play will consist of some twenty monologues on a variety of topics, a couple of short scenes, and pertinent musical acts. A genial announcer (Stage Manager) will be the key figure as he introduces both characters and musical acts. (My loose model is Garrison Keillor's "A Prairie Home Companion," but our show will deal exclusively with our own region. This format will lend itself to the Reader's Theatre approach wherein actors may use scripts as they did in radio days.) Such a plan will still require precise lighting and staging. The harmonica-piano interludes following each character's remarks will enhance what they said. (These will be brief and suggestive.)

The Stage Manager will set up the scenes borrowed from earlier plays. I suggest the following: the school scene from *ETR*, and the drug store scene from my World War II play, and a brief scene from the *New London* play. A separate area of the stage may be dedicated to these scenes with proper lighting and a few props. We will take an intermission about halfway through the material (a station-break, perhaps). Such a format will, I believe, result in a better flow of the play as one segment naturally proceeds to another. The play should last about two hours, including the intermission.

The characters will present their reminiscences in brief speeches ranging from three to five minutes. These people are drawing upon their own memories of an earlier period, as far back as the early 20th century and as recent as yesterday. Because they may be composites, the characters speak anonymously, identified only by what they are talking about. Hence, we have "The Teacher," "The Farmer," etc. They are united in a brief closing scene intended to show their mutuality across the years. (This will occur either during the curtain call or immediately after).

EAST TEXAS TALKS

ACT ONE

SCRIPT: *Time: 2009*

STAGE SETTING: *(A radio studio with microphones on stands, a stool and speaker's stand for the Host, eight chairs for characters behind microphone—perhaps two rows of four chairs,— and radio equipment table for sound effects man. The area for scenes from earlier plays will require a simple classroom with benches and a drugstore table and three chairs.) (These will be placed at the appropriate time.)*

(Lights down during announcer's introduction. Appropriate music plays and lights come up as S.M. enters for introductory remarks. He speaks from his podium. Music fades.)

AUTHOR/STAGE MANAGER: *(He is dressed in a sports jacket, dark pants, shirt with tie. He pulls tie knot down and opens collar button as he begins to speak into his microphone.)* Good evening to all our listeners out there in radio land. Welcome to another presentation of remembrances from East Texas, brought to you by the Lamp-Lite players from their playhouse located right here in beautiful Nacogdoches. We've got a live audience here, so that's why you'll be hearing laughter and applause. Our show is entitled *East Texas Talks* because that's what our characters will be doing—just talking about our part of the world. Oh, they'll be remembering, all right, but they might throw in a few comments just to spice things up. After all, this is Texas. Speaking of Texas, it's a big place, and sometimes you have to be a little more specific with regard to geography. There's North Texas, West Texas, and South Texas. And then there's East Texas with a capital "E." Folks in these parts were among the first settlers to come to Texas—if you don't count the native Americans and others who were already here (and we usually didn't). A few Anglo-Americans wandered in as early as about 1800, came right here to this area. Later, when Mexico opened up Texas to immigration, a lot more Americans came. That wasn't such a smart idea, because it wasn't long before the Texans rebelled and set up their own country for about ten years before the United States offered statehood in 1845. Several years later, the Texians—

as they are known—threw in with the Southern states and formed the Confederacy. That didn't last long either in view of the Civil War that erupted. By 1865 Texas found itself starting over again, but with all that land it had a bright future. A lot of people moving west passed through East Texas, but a lot of them settled here. By 1900, the state had about three million people. Well, that's enough history. It brings us down to about where we want to start our program: the early 20th century.

A few of our characters will comment on the early part of the century. Others will recall memorable events from the 1920s, '30s, and '40s, and on into the modern era. So, get ready to hear some down-home stories . . .

(Lights begin to fade on S.M., as a harmonica rendition of "Polly Wolly Doodle" begins.)

Oh, I meant to tell you—these people are representative of what they're talking about. We call the first character "The Centenarian" because he was a hundred years old when we caught up with him. He's just finished plowing up his garden with a mule . . .

(Stage goes dark as character moves to microphone.)

THE CENTENARIAN: *(He wears overalls, blue shirt, and straw hat.)* Yep, I been around for a long time. Don't know why the Lord's let me live so long. I've outlived all my family and friends, so there ain't much for me to do, except plow this plot of ground *(points to garden)*. See that mule there? I'm seven or eight times older than he is—I reckon I've had that mule for fifteen years—I don't even remember where I got him. That's how it is when you get old—can't remember yesterday, but I don't have much trouble remembering things that happened a long time ago. What'd you want to ask me about? The depression? Hell, boy, which one? I remember the hard times of the 1890s when Grover Cleveland was president. He never should have trusted those Republicans. All they wanted to do was corner the gold market. And, there was Teddy Roosevelt—he also presided over an economic downturn in 1907. They called 'em "panics" back then. Too much was happening too soon. That was about the time I was trying to feed my family by teaching school. But I learned quick that you'd never get ahead doing that, so I went into bidness myself—ran a store here in San Augustine and later got into buying cotton. A man could make a little money doing that—as long as the weather cooperated, and the markets held up. We had a lot of sharecropping and tenant farming here in East Texas back in those days—called it "farming on the thirds and fourths." When the crops came in, the farmer got a fraction of the income and the landowner got the rest. It was just a form of subsistence, but what else were they gonna do? They all had mouths to feed. They mainly grew cotton and corn. Corn was the gasoline of the day—mules have to eat, too. One guy summed it up this way: You grow the corn to feed the mule to pull the plow to grow the corn. You get the idea.

Things kind of rocked along there in the 1920s, kind of like my Model T Ford on that bumpy road to Nacogdoches. The stock market went into a boom back east, but that didn't matter much in these parts because most people didn't own any investments. When that thing crashed in 1929, it eventually brought the economy down. One fellow told me that he'd been in a depression all his life, so he wasn't worried about this one. People just expected hard times. They'd been livin' hand-to-mouth for half a century. They could make it as long as they had enough cornbread and a hog or two. Some people think I ought to sell this place and move into one of those homes for old folks, but I've got news for them: I ain't never gonna move! I'll just die right here—probably sittin' on these steps. *(He pauses as he speaks directly to audience.)* There're worse things than death.

(Lights fade as harmonica interlude comes up— "There's No Place Like Home.")

S.M.: *(Lights up on S.M., stage right.)* That's an interesting proposition. Who knows? Well, we're not gonna figure that out tonight. Our next character also had some vivid memories of early East Texas. She was a teacher who started out in a one-room school.

THE TEACHER: *(Lights up on a meek little woman. She wears a simple dress with a shawl as a wrap. Her hair is gray, and she wears old-fashioned, metal-rimmed glasses.)* Well, my life wasn't very exciting. I was just a country girl who became a schoolteacher. I was in high school when my family moved to East Texas—must have been in early 1918. I was born in 1900 in Collin County. My family were farmers, so we had to move around quite a bit. After we got here, I attended Nacogdoches High School—rode in a buggy with my sister and younger brother. We lived out toward Douglass. I never did graduate because there was a mix-up in my credits, but it didn't keep me from going to college. Actually, I taught in county schools for several years before

I started to college. My first job was in a one-teacher school—that was me—in the Palestine community right near our farm.

(As she speaks, the schoolroom set is prepared.)

That year nearly killed me—I had seven grades all by myself. I even had to get there early to clean the building and start a fire when it was cold. But I didn't quit. I later got about two years in college up in Denton by going summers. I know this sounds kind of crazy, but that's how most teachers did it in those days: taught during the year on a temporary certificate and attended college in the summers.

(At this point insert schoolroom scene. Young teacher enters before students. She mimes feeding of wood into a stove and dusting benches. Lively students enter as The Teacher watches from microphone. Scene ends with class going to lunch. The Teacher resumes her story from microphone.)

SCHOOL SCENE

EMILY: Here's the right answer, Dummy! 6 x 7 is 42, not 40, Dummy.

TOMMY: *(Pulls her pigtail.)* Who's a Dummy, Miss Smarty Pants—maybe that will pull some of that smart right out of your head!

ALL KIDS: Smarty, smarty had a party. Nobody came but Mr. Darby! Smarty, Sma—

TEACHER: Class! Class! Stop this nonsense and settle down. Every time I turn my back, you're up to mischief, Tommy!

TOMMY: She started it calling me a dummy!

EMILY: I did not! Cross my heart and hope to die!

TEACHER: All right, all right. Let's start with the Pledge of Allegiance. "I pledge allegiance to the flag of the United States of America and to the Republic for which it stands, one Nation, indivisible, with liberty and justice for all."

TEACHER: Now, who will begin the recitation of our memory work?

(Elizabeth raises hand.)

Elizabeth, will you recite the poem you learned by heart?

ELIZABETH: Yes, Miss Chapman. *(She recites poem.)*

TEACHER: Very good, Elizabeth! Now, who can say a new Bible verse?

JOE: I know one—"Jesus wept." Father says that's the shortest one! *(Kids laugh.)*

TEACHER: Who knows one a little longer?

BETTY: *(Waves hand.)* "Do unto others as you would have them do unto you." That's the Golden Rule.

TEACHER: Yes, that is the Golden Rule. Let's recite that all together. *(Children recite.)* Now, who can recite the first ten presidents?

CAROLINE: Washington, Adams, Jefferson, Madison, Monroe, Adams, Jackson, Van Buren, Harrison, Tyler.

TEACHER: Very good, Caroline. Now until lunch we will work on our multiplication tables "by rote." 2 x 2 is 4; 2 x 3 is 6; 2 x 4 *(etc.)*

(Freeze.)

Time for lunch, children. *(Children start outside with syrup buckets.)*

BOY: I got a sweet potato.

ANOTHER CHILD: I've got a biscuit with molasses—want to swap?

TOMMY: Let's play Red Rover.

BILLY: No, let's play Pop the Whip!

TEACHER: *(resumes)* After SFA opened in 1923, I decided to get my degree there—started in 1924. Sooner or later you had to attend a long term. I stayed at home for a while—drove my father's Model T Ford up to the campus on the north edge of town. Never could back that thing up! Later, I moved to town and got me a room. I walked everywhere I went. I remember one girl who got in trouble for taking the screen off her boarding house window. When the dean of women found out and asked her why she did that, she said, "I do not like my air screened." *(She laughs.)* Everyone knew she was slipping out at night. I didn't have time for that kind of thing. I worked in the library and played basketball. Then I walked back to my boarding house . . . *(Proudly)* I got my degree in the first graduating class in 1925. After that, I taught at various East Texas schools. I got my master's at Peabody College in 1930. I retired after more than 40 years in the public schools. *(Pauses and looks away.)* It seems like yesterday . . . I don't know what they're teaching these kids today—not much from what I can tell. Now, I don't mean to be critical of teachers. I'm on their side. But life just seems to be moving too fast. Kids are too distracted. I've been retired more than 30 years, and since then I've been to Europe, Alaska, the west coast, but you don't want to know about that . . . Like I said, my life hasn't been very exciting.

(Lights down on Teacher as harmonica plays "School Days.")

S.M.: *(At podium)* Some life! That woman's been farther than I have. You know, teachers sometimes don't know just how much influence they had on all those students. It reminds me of our next character, "The Professor." He taught for nearly 40 years in a state college—not unlike the one we have in our town. Listen to his story.

THE PROFESSOR: *(Lights up on microphone. He wears a sports coat, shirt and bow tie.)* I've realized that professors are often seen as "strange ducks." Anyone who makes a living teaching a few hours a week for a nine-month term is suspect to those who work longer hours for less money. In reality, professors work far more than you might think—class preparation, grading exams, conference sessions, and committee meetings, just to mention a few of the professor's duties. On top of that, he has to worry about the dean and pushy parents who can't understand why Susie made a "D." If he's conscientious, he'll also be working on scholarly stuff, too, like traveling around East Texas interviewing people. It all takes time and effort. As for getting the summer off, I don't know what that means. Most of us teach summer school to make ends meet financially, and we're lucky if we find a little time to work on scholarly things . . . and the pay is not that great, either. Do you know many professors who make as much money as a beginning medical doctor? Yet they spend roughly the same amount of time preparing for their professional status.

Now, mind you, I'm not complaining—just explaining. In the long run, professing is a wonderful way to spend a lifetime because you have a chance to influence how students think. After thirty or so years, professors amass a vast number of former students. (Do the arithmetic: 300 students a year for 35 years equals more than 10,000 students.) It's nice to know that you've touched the lives of so many people—well, maybe some of them. I'll admit that 18-year-olds aren't always the best vessels to pour literature or history into. But you'd be surprised how many students eventually wish they knew more about how things work. By the time they're a little older, you know the story about the kid who realized how much his parents learned after he or she had been away for a while. *(He chuckles.)* Well, that's the way it is with teaching. *(Pauses)* It's a noble profession.

(Lights down on Professor while harmonica plays alma-mater-like tune, perhaps "Hail to SFA.")

S.M.: *(Lights up on podium.)* Sounds like a good racket to me. Finding a job, you like is important. In fact, just getting a job proved to be a major accomplishment during the depression. Fortunately for this area, the great East Texas Oil Boom came in with a mighty roar in 1930. It was located mainly in Rusk and Gregg counties, just north of here. Thousands of people poured into the region—most of them looking for a job. It was a godsend for many, like our next character: the "Oil Field Hand."

OIL FIELD HAND: *(He saunters to microphone to tune of "Oh Susannah" on harmonica. He is wearing khaki pants and shirt with a felt hat pushed back on his head.)* I come down from Oklahoma in May of '31. Caught a ride on a milk truck just south of the Red River and came on in to Kilgore—got in about midnight. I spent the first night in a tent with a bunch of cots in it; cost me a quarter. When I got up the next morning, I ate breakfast in a little board shack café in the middle of present Kilgore. It was a good deal—you could eat for 35 cents. Within a few days, I got a job roughnecking on a rig—mainly because I had a few contacts from my experience in the Oklahoma oil fields. I made six dollars a day for a 12-hour shift. You worked from 12 to 12, one way or the other. It was a hard job; when I wasn't workin' I was sleepin' or tryin' to get to work. Roads were virtually impassable at times because it was so muddy—I've seen Caterpillar tractors buried up to the exhaust pipes on the streets of Kilgore. This field was fairly easy to drill because it was pretty shallow. But the secret to success was having a good crew. One guy told me that his crew could complete a well in eight hours, but I never did believe him. There were four roughnecks plus a driller—five men to a crew. Everyone had a nickname—"blondie, blackie, slim or shortie." You had to be careful around all that equipment—it was dangerous, and I can testify that it was hard work. But people had a mind to work back then—none of this 'moochin' and marchin' like we hear of today. I finally got on with "the company" in the fall of '32, and that was a much better job. It cut my workday to eight hours. Yes, sir, I spent more than 30 years with the "company." Best thing that ever happened to me.

The worst thing I ever saw in East Texas was when that school blew up in New London. I had a brother-in-law who lived over there—he worked all night helpin' to get those bodies out. It bothered him for years. I'll tell you, that disaster ruined a lot of lives. How would you feel if your kid didn't come home from school?

(Lights fade as he stares into space. A mournful harmonica rendition of "Red Sails in the Sunset.")

S.M.: *(Lights slowly up on S.M. as he introduces next scene while transitioning into Preacher.)*

THE PREACHER: We don't know how we would have felt because we weren't there. That's why I want you to pay careful attention to our next character. *(He puts coat on stool and moves to other microphone.)* He was there. *(Pauses)* When I woke up that dreadful day in 1937, I had no idea of what I was about to face. It was early spring, the birds were singin' and the world seemed right with God. *(Another pause)* Later on, while I was working on my Sunday sermon in the church study, I heard a loud explosion. It was a little after 3 p.m. I ran outside and saw a huge cloud over the school. The world had turned dark.

I got to the campus in about five minutes. I couldn't believe what I saw. The whole building was just a pile of rubble. Very little was left standing. A few people were wandering around in a daze, including some of the students. It wasn't long before help arrived—those oil field workers went straight to work, with their bosses right beside 'em. The most pitiful sight was those parents who rushed in, looking for their kids. I stayed there most of the night, helping with the recovery and trying to comfort people. They strung up lights, so the workers could see. Got home about dawn the next morning, cleaned up, and started planning funerals. The next few days were kind of hazy. I reckon I did—oh, at least thirty funerals. We held some of 'em in the church, but a good many were graveside services—right there in that cemetery between here and Henderson. *(Chorus softly performs "In the Sweet Bye and Bye.")* Once we got past the shock, people began to settle down. School started up within a couple of weeks. The children seemed to handle it pretty good, but the grown-ups had a hard time coping with it. There wasn't much joy around here for a long time, as a lot of people can testify. *(He stands aside as the next character speaks.)*

NEW LONDON SCENE

BONNIE JONES: *(She is a middle-aged woman wearing a simple but nice dress.)* I'm Bonnie Jones. We lived in New London when that school blew up. We had a little house about two miles from the school. I was sitting on the back porch talking with a neighbor-lady when we heard this loud sound. It startled me, but my friend said it was probably just a boiler exploding out in the oil field. Well, we stepped out into the yard and saw a big cloud in the air off in the direction of the school. *(She pauses to gather herself.)* I had a terrible sinking feeling. All I could think about was our son, Gary. I ran down to meet him at the bus stop, like I always did. As soon as he got off the bus, he told me that he saw the school blow up. Later a friend dropped by and said my husband Harry had gone up there to help out. I didn't see him until about ten o'clock the next morning.

I didn't sleep much that night. My husband was terribly upset when he got home the next day. His clothes were all dirty and torn, and he had a hard time talking. He barely ate or slept for several weeks because he couldn't get it off his mind. He had a lot of stomach trouble. Just driving by the school brought it all back. That's why he kept putting in for a transfer. We eventually moved away. *(Lights down on Bonnie.)*

PREACHER: *(He returns to microphone as Bonnie steps aside.)* Many years later two victims of this disaster met at a community reunion. One of them was her husband, Harry, and the other was George Willet, a high school student injured in the explosion. They had a lot to talk about. Let's listen in. . . .

(As Preacher speaks, the two friends greet each other, center stage front.)

GEORGE: Harry, Harry Jones! Is that you? Are you still playing baseball?

(They shake hands.)

HARRY: George Willet! I was hoping that you'd be at this reunion. Last I heard, you'd wandered somewhere out west.

GEORGE: Well, I came back. You can't stay away forever. Time changes things.

HARRY: It sure does. *(Pauses)* Remember when I visited you over there in the hospital?

GEORGE: How could I forget? You told me to hang on—that there was a reason why I survived. Well, I'm still hanging on. How's your boy?

HARRY: Which one?

GEORGE: The one who had polio?

HARRY: How'd you know about that? We moved away.

GEORGE: Oh, I was working down there not far from Houston and heard about your son—they said he needed blood of a certain type—the same as mine. So, I went to the hospital and donated, but I didn't get to see you. I moved to West Texas soon after that, so I kind of lost touch. I knew he'd survive, though, because he had a pint of my blood and I'm a survivor. You told me I'd understand some day.

HARRY: *(He speaks slowly with some difficulty.)* That boy is fine, George. He'll turn 42 years old this fall. *(To audience.)* Now, I understand.

(George puts his arm around Harry's shoulder and they slowly begin to walk off but freeze with spot on them stage right center. Bonnie joins them. Piano softly plays "London, Oh London.")

S.M.: *(Lights up on Preacher as he moves back to his microphone and puts jacket on, which re-establishes him as S.M. again.)*

(Lights up on S.M. as he introduces Ab Allen to sing "Precious Lord.")

Here's Ab Allen with a song used at some of those funerals, "Precious Lord, Take My Hand."

(Ab sings.)

S.M.: Thank you there, Brother Ab. That tragedy left its mark on East Texas—and the world. If you ever get a chance to visit the site in Rusk County, stop and spend a few minutes reading the names on the monument that stands in front of the rebuilt school. It's located on state highway 42, about 10 miles northeast of Henderson. And be sure to visit the museum just across the street. *(Pauses)* In a way, that event foreshadowed the coming of World War II a few years later. It was a microcosm of the death and destruction that plagued the world from 1939 to 1945. You'd be right if you think that's my transition into the Second World War, the greatest event of the 20th century. The next two characters are prime examples of how that conflict affected millions of Americans, and they both came from Nacogdoches County.

THE PATRIOT: *(Lights up on an older man—a little bent. He speaks with an East Texas accent—a little haltingly. He wears khaki pants, plain shirt, and VFW cap.)* I was born in East Texas and grew up out there in the Harmony community just west of Nacogdoches. That time I was born in—you see, I was born in 1919, not long after the First World War ended—it wasn't anything like it is today. We lived on a farm and tried to grow cotton, had a few head of cattle. The roads weren't very good then—we was lucky if we got to town once a month. We had what we needed to eat, but we didn't have much money. After that Depression hit in the early '30's, times got even harder. If it hadn't been for some of those programs Franklin Roosevelt started, I don't know what would have happened. Anyhow, I went to about the tenth grade in school, which was pretty good. I didn't know it then, but I was about to get a real education after I joined the army in 1937.

My first assignment was with the horse cavalry in South Texas. They paid me $21 a month to help patrol along the Mexican border; they fed us well. Then I went to an artillery unit at Fort Sam Houston. In the spring of 1940, we shipped out for the Philippine Islands—left out of San Francisco on the *USS Grant*. It took us about 20 days to get there, see. We ended up in Manila. That's where I was when the Japanese bombed Pearl Harbor. I knew we were headed for a war, but I also knew that the Lord would take care of me, regardless of what happened. Well, I volunteered to take supplies down to the Bataan Peninsula in the southern part of the Philippines. We left Manila on Christmas Eve of 1941 and hooked up with an infantry unit. Things just got worse.

The Japanese eventually backed us up to the water, see, I mean there wasn't anywhere to go. As it turned out, we ran out of food, water, and ammunition, and *(pauses)*, hope. I knew what was gonna happen. We were down to a bowl of rice a day, and most of us were plagued by malaria. I finally wandered down a jungle trail right into the hands of the enemy. The only thing more numerous was green flies, by the millions. We couldn't do anything but surrender. I was captured on the tenth of April 1942. What lay ahead, see, was that terrible march out of Bataan. I never saw so much suffering in my life. Then we were crowded into boxcars that took us to a POW camp. I just lived from minute to minute. I stayed there for about a year before I was shipped to Japan.

Well, I ended up in prison camp #17 at Omuta, on the island of Kyushu—about 30 miles from Nagasaki. That's where I spent the rest of the war, working in the coal mines. They nearly worked us to death, see, and we didn't have much food or medical care. I received no mail while I was there—from the middle of 1943 until the war ended in August of 1945. Toward the end of the war, we could tell that it was winding down because of the American bombers going over. The guards finally ran away, and we took over the camp. I weighed about 120 pounds when I was liberated. *(Pause)* But I always felt that I would survive—in other words, I never gave up. But it wasn't my doing—it was the Lord who took care of me. I don't think I have any hatred for the Japanese people, but I don't want much to do with 'em. In other words, I don't buy any Japanese cars. I helped raise the American flag over that camp after we were liberated. I'm telling you, it was a moving experience.

(Lights fade as harmonica plays "America, the Beautiful" and actor returns to chair.)

S.M.: *(Pauses to let words sink in. Then he introduces the drug store scene.)* That war affected every person in this country, especially women who sat around waiting for letters from their loved ones all over the world. After checking the mail at the post office, a group of women over in Alto went to Boyd's drug store to discuss their woes. Let's listen in. Here's Mabel Clifton.

MABEL CLIFTON: My husband was drafted before the war began. He was sent to Ft. Benning, Georgia, and I followed him down there with two kids. It was hard to find a place to live around Ft. Benning. We ended up living in a three-room milk cooler located on a farm near there—that's just how hard it was to find a place to live. We had rats so big that we would shoot them with BB guns. We had gone to the movie on that Sunday when the war began. Now my grandmother and mother were quite religious, and they had always taught me you shouldn't go to the movie on Sunday. We came out and I heard about that war, I thought I had caused it! But my husband quickly convinced me that it wasn't my fault. *(She chuckles.)* After he went overseas, I returned to my hometown of Alto, Texas. By now we had a young son, in addition to my two daughters. I was able to live in my mother's house and we got along okay. A group of us "War Widows" would meet every morning at the Post Office to check on our mail and see if we had any news. Then we would go down the street to Boyd's Drug Store where we would sit and drink Cokes.

(Stage Direction: Scene shifts to Boyd's Drug Store in Alto, Texas. There will be a table with several women sitting around. As scene opens, they are talking and laughing. One woman wears a white apron—Mrs. Boyd. She serves Cokes. As Mabel Clifton enters, others greet her.)

MRS. BOYD: 'Morning, Mabel. Did you get any news today?

MABEL: *(Mabel sits down at table while talking.)* No letter today, but I got two yesterday. It's the same old stuff—no news. Those censors won't let them tell anything. Boy, I'll be glad when this war is over!

SECOND WOMAN: Mrs. Boyd, I need to fix up a package for my husband. He needs some soap and razorblades, and put in a few of those peanut patties, please. He says he's tired of all those chocolate bars they get.

MABEL: Does anyone have any extra sugar stamps? I need to bake a birthday cake for my son. This rationing sure does cramp my style.

THIRD WOMAN: I've got a few stamps you can have. Remember how I was wanting a shoe stamp last week? My daughter needed a new pair of shoes for her piano recital. Poor little thing—her toes were sticking out. Well, I went up to the rationing board—took her along to show them how bad she needed shoes. 'Course, I took the worst pair and showed them. I got the stamp, though, but now I can't find shoes anywhere. Guess I'll have to go over to Nacogdoches, if I've got enough gas to get there.

MABEL: *(Laughing)* Well, here we are griping about shortages again, while our husbands are off fighting for us. What a war!

(Lights fade on drug store scene and scene returns to reader.)

MABEL: All we could do was just wait. I believe the war brought us all together. Sure, there was a lot of greed and a lot of those "4-F's" tried to take advantage of us "War Widows." Generally, people got along and pulled together. I always felt like my husband was off doing a job and what I had to do was to keep the home together. And I think that at least 90% of the people felt that way.

(As scene ends, Tom Nader enters to perform two war era songs, "I'll Be Seeing You" and "Pistol-Packing Mama.")

(As singing ends, S.M. introduces next character.)

S.M.: Thank you, Tom. The other veteran went the other way in World War II. He served in the European theater and then came home to pick up where he left off. Let's welcome "The Pragmatist," because that's what he was, during the war and afterwards.

THE PRAGMATIST: *(Lights up on a large black man. He stands straight, suggesting the stance of an athlete. His voice is strong. He is dressed in sweat pants and sweatshirt topped by a Dragon cap.)* My view of the war was a lot different from what that poor guy had to endure in the Pacific. I was born in Nacogdoches in 1920, one of nine children. I started school in 1927. We had segregated schools in those days, but I got a pretty good education. 'Course, I spent a lot of time playing football, and it paid off: I got a scholarship to play ball up at Texas College in Tyler. It was hard work—those coaches got us up at 5 a.m. and made us run several miles before breakfast. They demanded discipline. I played guard both ways—offense and defense. We had a good team—I'll never forget when we played Tuskegee in a bowl game over there in Birmingham—we beat 'em 13 to 12.

About that time, the war came along. Like many of my fellow students, I joined the enlisted reserve. We were called up a year later and sent up to Fort Sill in Oklahoma to train in the field artillery. We were later put in the 777th battalion and sent to California for more training. It was an all-black unit—mainly students from black colleges. My interest in mathematics got me assigned to the headquarters company as a computer. I helped to aim those big guns that could send a 65-pound shell twenty miles away. We shipped out from Boston in early 1944, just in time to get in on the invasion of Europe. We went through Normandy about three weeks after the big day. Part of it was still smoking. Our unit participated in the big sweep into Germany—went through parts of Holland and Belgium before we crossed the River Rhine. Being part of the artillery, we weren't right on the front line, but it wasn't far away. I saw a lot of bodies, and it bothered me. I ended up in Austria after the European part of the war ended in the spring of 1945. Most of us expected to be sent to the Pacific, but the Japanese surrendered, and we came home—rode on the *Queen Mary*. I was back at Texas College playing football in 1946. When I graduated in 1948, I had thirteen coaching offers, but I chose to come back to Nacogdoches. I ended up as head coach at the black high school. We had good teams.

War changes things! Racial segregation was still in place when I left for the war, but when I came home, I could see some cracks in the system. Black people had moved around a lot. They went all over the country to find war jobs, and things slowly began to change. When school integration finally came to East Texas in the mid-1960s, we had a few problems, but people learned that they could work together. I went to Nacogdoches High School as an assistant coach and finished out my career. I enjoyed my work with young people. Later, I served on the school board and helped to solve some of those problems. It was kind of like doing math, one step at a time. We just had to be patient.

(Lights down on coach. Harmonica plays "We Shall Overcome.")

S.M.: *(Lights up on S.M. who introduces next character.)* Blacks weren't the only group that experienced discrimination in earlier times. Women also felt left out, especially when it came to getting jobs. They really took up the slack during the war because so many men were serving in the military. Our next character found herself in something of a quandary when she tried to hang on to a job she got during World War II. You remember "Rosie the Riveter." We'll call her "Polly, the Papermaker." Here's her story.

THE PAPERMAKER: *(Lights up on a jolly woman in jeans and a checked shirt. She is in her seventies.)* I lived down on the coast for a couple of years before I came home to East Texas. I needed to take care of my aging parents toward the end of the war—my brothers were off in the service. Well, there was this paper mill in my hometown, so I went out there and applied for a job. I was lucky—got a job testing samples in the laboratory. Papermaking was new to this area. They even had to import skilled workers from Canada and up north who knew how to make paper. Boy, did we ever fool them. A lot of those people didn't think East Texans—especially women—could do that kind of work. I wasn't married at the time, and I needed a job. I had to work the night shift, but that didn't matter to me. I also had to go out and get those samples. I crawled all over that equipment. Actually, the lab had several women doing what I did, but most of 'em decided to quit when the boys came home. I guess I shocked the bosses, but I didn't want to quit. The pay was pretty good, so I just stayed there. In fact, I stayed until I retired thirty years later. I worked as hard as any man in that plant, and they knew it. But I made lots of friends out there, and I later married one of those papermakers. It was the best time of my life! Who said women should stay at home?

(Lights down as harmonica plays "Get Out in that Kitchen and Rattle Those Pots and Pans.")

S.M.: *(Lights up as S.M. bops to music; he chuckles as he introduces next speaker.)* This next guy didn't have to worry about losing his job to returning World War II veterans. He was one of them! But he had a hand in creating some new jobs. He came from a long line of farmers who were always looking for something to grow. He didn't know it at the time, but he was a pioneer in the chicken business that eventually became the heart of East Texas agriculture. We'll call him "The Farmer."

THE FARMER: *(Lights up on a heavy-set man dressed in jeans and shirt, plus a cowboy hat. He speaks in a deep East Texas twang.)* I've been involved in agriculture all my life, except for that little vacation in Europe during the 1940s. My family came to East Texas after the Civil War—run out of Alabama by hard times. In fact, I still live on land they bought for 50 cents an acre. Cotton was the big crop here until the coming of the Depression and the war. At one time, Nacogdoches County had more than 20 cotton gins. Sharecroppers still played a big role in the local economy, but as times changed people began to move off. A lot of them eventually went to work in defense plants down on the coast, and a bunch of us went off to the war itself. Cotton eventually moved to West Texas and the Panhandle, leaving East Texas farmers without a main crop. What we needed was some kind of agriculture that would appeal to land owners who wanted to stay on the farm.

Well, like I said, I went off to the war in 1943—served in the field artillery over there in Europe. We had the Germans on the run when I got there in 1944, but I'll never forget one scene we came across. It was a concentration camp. I can still see those refugees;

they had hollow, sunken eyes. And there were ditches full of rotting bodies. At one point, I just sat down and cried. I promised the Lord that if I got through that war I'd never complain. Well, I got back all right—returned to Nacogdoches County in 1946. My father owned a little Purina feed store, and I just went into business with him.

Along there in the late 1940s, someone got the idea that this region would be suited to growing poultry—chickens. They'd already tried it over in Shelby County, and it worked. Thanks to some leading citizens, we decided to give it a try over here. My dad and I sold a lot of feed in fifty-pound bags to those early growers. They had little 300 capacity houses, see. I remember one little old woman who borrowed $900 to build her first house, and it worried her having that much debt. She later sold her first batch of chickens for over a thousand dollars and became one of our best customers. These were small operations, you see, but pretty soon we had an industry going. Companies came in and built processing plants and truckers made a lot of money hauling chickens. Before long we had an integrated business right here—from hatcheries to big chicken houses that handled thousands of birds at a time. They're ready for the packing plant in about eight weeks. It just mushroomed here! Do you realize that about a million birds a day are processed within a forty-mile radius of Nacogdoches? That's a lot of fried chicken.

(Lights down on The Farmer. Musical interlude as harmonica plays "Old McDonald Had a Farm." Sound of chickens clucking as musical interlude ends.)

S.M.: Well, it's time for a station break, folks, so we'll take a little intermission. Don't forget to flush. We'll be right back in a few minutes.

(House lights up as Act One ends.)

INTERMISSION

ACT TWO

S.M.: *(Appropriate music over house sound system as lights come up on Act Two.)* Welcome back to *East Texas Talks* from the stage of the Lamp-Lite Playhouse here in Nacogdoches. We were talking about chickens when we left off. They weren't the only newcomers to East Texas in those post-war years. People also moved here from elsewhere, including some Yankees and other foreigners. These outsiders likely underwent considerable "culture shock" until they realized what this area was all about. (Maybe, not quite so shocking as what happened to the chickens.) Now, East Texas people are nearly always polite, but some of them can be a little cool to strangers. If you weren't born here—I trust you've heard about the "B.I.N."s? (That's "born in Nacogdoches.) It reminds me of one fellow I knew: He'd lived here for 50 years—an important leader in the community. At his funeral—a real first-class one, I'd say—someone was heard to remark, "Oh, he was an outsider, you know, born in West Texas." Well, the next character was born there, too, but that's a plus, because he can offer a little perspective on the two regions. Welcome "The Outsider."

THE OUTSIDER: *(Lights up on a tall man who ambles up to microphone wearing a western jacket and big cowboy hat.)* I wouldn't call myself an outsider, although it's true I wasn't born here. Now, I could say that I got here as soon as I could, but that probably won't satisfy some people. Yep, I'm from West Texas, that wonderful, wide-open place where you can actually see the stars at night. It's quite different from here, but I can't help where I was born.

One of the first things I noticed after moving to East Texas some 25 years ago was the language barrier—and I'm not talking about any foreign language! I thought I spoke English when I got here, but I couldn't understand some of these East Texans. They seemed to have their own dialect. Maybe it's because many of them were Southern in background—whatever, they seem to drag out their words into several syllables. Have you ever noticed how some of these East Texas people pronounce the word "war?" They can get two or three syllables out of that! And you're not always sure which war "(wa-ar)" they're talking about. Chances are it's the civil conflict that happened over a hundred years ago. Some of 'em are still fighting it, too.

Now, I don't want to be critical, but I believe East Texans are more clannish than people from my part of the state. That's probably due to the fact that they tended to stay put—didn't move around so much. Kids got to know their grandparents and the whole "family tree" thing. You can learn a lot by visiting the little cemeteries out in the country. A lot of 'em are near church buildings.

Which brings up the topic of religion—it's taken quite seriously in these parts. Have you ever counted the number of Baptist churches in this area? There must be several hundred if you count all the different varieties. Now, it's not for me to say if religion made saints out of everyone, but it definitely made an impact on people's lives. We had a lot of churches in West Texas, too—all flavors, but not so numerous. It reminds me of the writer who said that, "God went to church every Wednesday night in West Texas." He also wore suits from J.C. Penney's. *(He laughs.)*

As for politics, I can't see much difference between the two regions. Almost everybody seems to be Republican these days. I can remember when that wasn't the case. You found a whole lot more Democrats back during the Depression in the 1930s. Why, Franklin D. Roosevelt was almost next to God when times were hard. Time changes things, don't it?

Although I made my living in the oil fields (they've got oil fields out there, too), I confess that I spent a little time "cowboyin'." You know, big hats and boots? But it's always seemed to me that East Texas cowboys are more drawn to the glamour of the profession. They want bigger hats and belt buckles.

In conclusion, I can say that I like both regions. I eventually got used to all these big trees over here, unlike my little daddy who said the forests made him nervous. He preferred West Texas because you could see farther. Maybe he didn't want anybody sneakin' up on him. I thank you for your attention.

(Removes hat and bows sweepingly. Lights down on Outsider. Tune: "Don't Fence Me In.")

S.M.: *(Lights up on S.M.. He looks around sneakily.)* Oh, to see ourselves as others see us—Robert Burns, "To a Louse." That's what I like about poetry: it reduces things to a few words. Now, the next character must have been a poet at heart, because he has an uncanny way of looking at East Texas from another view. He's an "insider."

THE INSIDER: *(Lights up on a well but casually dressed man with a sparkle in his eye.)* Heavens to Betsy! I don't know why I'm up here talking about East Texas. Maybe it's because I have a reputation as a big mouth. I do know a little bit about this part of the world, seeing as I was born right here in Nacogdoches more than 70 years ago. Not everyone can claim to be a "B.I.N." Now, let me point out that Nacogdoches is the cultural capital of Deep East Texas. It's also recognized far and wide as the oldest town in the state. Of course, a few other burgs might have some claim to that title—like San Antonio, El Paso, or even San Augustine—but they don't talk about it as much as we do. I realize that a lot of people—especially historians—sometimes dismiss this as chamber of commerce hype, but they can't prove it's not true, if you get what I mean. I guess it's just part of the Texas mystique.

Those of us privileged to live here realize that we have a particular point of view, which, I admit, may not always be as progressive as some of us might wish. For instance, we might be a little prone to living in the past—you know, wanting things to stay as they always were. And, we're sometimes reluctant to accept outsiders, even though it's obvious that some of our best-known citizens came from somewhere else. But in the long run, it usually works out, like when we got the college more than 80 years ago. Where would we be without the college? Why, we'd be San Augustine or Center, or even Lufkin, heaven forbid. Nacogdoches has this thing about Lufkin. Oh, it's a nice town but a little seedy in places. *(He grimaces.)* If it weren't for high school football, they wouldn't have much to brag about. Well, there's some nice stores over there, and the place does seem to be growing. *(He gestures with hand.)* But we've got more culture in Nacogdoches. There's all those nice old buildings that haven't been torn down yet, not to mention the Old Stone Fort. It was an eyesore before they razed it in the early 20th century. Some people said it even smelled bad. It finally came to rest out at the college when it was re-constructed in the 1930s. I understand they even used some of the original stones. Actually, *(an aside)* it's a replica, but most people don't know that. *(He puts tongue in cheek.)*

By now, you've probably realized that I'm just joshing you. *(He smiles.)* I could talk all night about East Texas and Nacogdoches. On the one hand, this is a good place to live if you don't mind the heat, mosquitoes, poison ivy, hay fever, pine pollen, drought, hurricanes, floods and other assorted flukes of nature. On the other hand, it's a beautiful place filled with wonderful people. In short, I like it so well that I've got a burial plot in Oak Grove Cemetery; you can consider that my permanent address. I bid you good evening.

(Lights down on speaker as he bows. Harmonica concludes with "Shave and a Haircut Six Bits.")

S.M.: *(Lights up on S.M.)* Texas mystique? Maybe that explains our tendency to brag. *(Pause for comment to sink in).* Now, our next speaker had a hard time adjusting to the Texas heat. Her views are reminiscent of that old saying, "If I owned both Texas and hell, I'd rent out Texas and live in hell," but I suspect she'd have an entirely different outlook. Welcome the "War Bride."

THE WAR BRIDE: *(Lights up on a slender woman in her mid-sixties. She wears jeans and a bright shirt. She holds a tack hammer in her hands. She speaks in a soft British accent.)* Well, I wouldn't say that I welcomed the Texas heat. It was the worst thing I had to deal with in the first few years of my life in East Texas. I thought I'd been deposited in Hades. But for a girl who'd experienced the blitz in London, it wasn't so bad. Those times in 1940, soon after World War II began, were just terrible. In fact, my sister and I were among the children removed from London for a few months. We were sent to the town of Bath, many miles from home. I was sick much of the time, so I ended up back in London after a few months. I later trained as an upholsterer. *(She shows hammer.)*

I didn't like the Yanks at first—they were so self-confident—a bunch of big talkers and showoffs. We saw a lot of them, but I didn't meet very many. But when I met *him*, he wasn't that way. We met when a girlfriend and I were on holiday near an American base north of London. It was a bit of a happenstance, really. We were riding bicycles near the base and *he* noticed me. I guess it was love at first sight. We exchanged letters, and he came to see me in the city. Before long, we decided to get married—but first he had to get approval from the military, and I had to convince my parents. It all worked out eventually, and we lived near the base for a while. He was a sergeant, in charge of a group of mechanics who kept those American airplanes flying. When the war ended, he had to return home, leaving me to come later, but by that time we were three. The baby and I finally arrived at New York City early in 1946, following a hectic and rough voyage of ten days. I later learned that I was one of about a million war brides who came here after the war.

New York City was fine, but I was keen to see Texas. My husband met us, and we were soon enroute to Marshall by train, where his family were waiting. Then it was on to Panola County, my new home. The road may have been unpaved, and the house had no running water, but it became my home. Sure, I missed my homeland and especially my parents, but America adopted me. I didn't get to see my folks for nearly ten years, but I didn't regret coming here. The U.S.A. proved to be a land of opportunity. We had six children, and I even got to put my early training to work. I set up an upholstery shop behind my house, and I did quite well, thank you very much. It's been an adventure living in East Texas, but I'm glad I came here to live among some of the best people in the world.

(Lights down on War Bride, as harmonica or ensemble performs "Beautiful, Beautiful Texas.")

S.M.: Let's give our speakers a rest while we listen to a little music. Or, as the country singers say, "It's time for our sacred number." Religious music goes way back in Southern culture. *(As he speaks, chairs are being arranged in a square for the Sacred Harp singers.)* One tradition that dates from a couple of centuries ago is Sacred Harp singing. It's also known as "fa-sol-la" music after the shaped notes they use. I'll let them tell you what they're going to do right here on "our stage" as Ed Sullivan used to say. Welcome the singing Wright Family and Friends from Kennard, Texas.

(A spokesman briefly explains about the Sacred Harp style.)

(Sacred Harp group performs.)

S.M.: Let's hear it for the Wright Family and Friends. I don't know much about that fa-sol-la stuff, but I'm quite impressed by Sacred Harp singing. It's got a real old-timey sound. Our next group also does religious music in a different way. They sing gospel music in the Stamps-Baxter style—that's a form of music that rose to popularity with the coming of radio back in the twenties. It's known for its lively rhythm which traditionalists often call "gospel boogie-woogie." Here are the "Gospelorians,"

(Gospelorians perform.)

S.M.: Would you believe that group's composed of four SFA professors and two employees of the music department? Let's get back to the program. Our next character also defied the norm. As we've already seen, strong women seem to be plentiful in East Texas. Maybe it's because society demands more of women. They bear the children, raise 'em, help earn a living, take care of the house and often run the church. That old adage is true—"a woman's work is never done." *(He introduces the next character, a black woman in her 80's.)* Our next character is proof of that. We call her "The Organizer."

THE ORGANIZER: *(She wears a fancy dress and a neat hat. She blinks several times and then speaks.)* These lights are a little bright in my eyes, but I think I can see you out there—at least I hear you breathin'. I took my first breath way back in 1921, when I was born near Nat out in the western part of the county. I was one of fifteen children—ten girls and five boys. My parents were poor sharecroppers and we didn't have much of this world's goods. In fact, my father was born in 1865 soon after my people were freed from slavery. But you know what? *(She points with finger.)* We had love and family, and those memories are very dear to me. We also had schools and the church to guide us toward being good citizens. I'll never forget that little country school in our community. It wasn't much to look at, but we learned to read and write, something my father never had the opportunity to enjoy. Later, we moved nearer Nacogdoches, so we could get further schooling. I finally graduated from E.J. Campbell and much later went on to Stephen F. Austin where I studied sociology. I wanted to learn how people can live and work together because that's what community means. Later, I got to try out some of those ideas as a social worker and teacher.

Now, I don't mean to sound like a preacher, but we had some problems along the way. We had to get rid of that old segregation system because it kept us from being a true community where people could work together. It wasn't easy. We had a lot of problems, but I want to say that this country and this community stood up to those hard times. I'm proud that I got to be a part of that process, although I have to say that I didn't enjoy all of those meetings. But the fact that we endured is a precious memory to me, and I'll always believe that we got a better community out of all that hard work. I served on committees, worked in the church, and even ran a program to preserve the history of my people. Along the way, I raised my own family and took a special interest in young people, because that's the key to building pride and preparing for the future. I never gave up on those kids. It was hard with all the problems that kids face today, but we got through it. Now I'm ready to go home—my feet are killin' me.

(Lights down as she leaves stage. Harmonica plays "Going Home.")

S.M.: *(Lights up on S.M. as he introduces the next speaker.)* Would you believe that East Texas experienced a fur boom in the 1970s and '80s? I'm talking about raccoons, foxes, bobcats—you know, the skins they use to make fur coats. *(Aside)* Not that many people need such garments here in the southland. It was reminiscent of the Rocky Mountains a long time ago when beaver skins were the pelts of choice. Fast forward a hundred and fifty years or so—you get the picture: History repeats itself. The fur buyer played an important role in that process. Here's how he explained it.

THE FUR MAN: *(Lights up. A skinny man about 40 years old, wears jeans, a cowboy shirt, and a western hat. He ambles to microphone, sizes up the audience, and begins to speak.)* I was born to be a fur buyer. My granddaddy started buying skins when he was a young man in the early 1900's over near Alto, and now I'm the third generation to carry on. My daddy came home from World War II just a'rarin' to get back to buying furs. He expanded throughout East Texas and even traveled over toward Louisiana and into the Hill Country. He almost cornered the market on ringtail cats one season—that's a raccoon-like animal widely found in central and west Texas. It's a valuable fur, but the common raccoon really drove the recent market. One season in the late 1970s when the boom was going good, Texas produced about a half million raccoon skins. At an averge price of about $26, those critters brought in a lot of money—now you figure on a cheap Chinese calculator and you get about $13 million. And the eastern half of Texas furnished about 95 per cent of those skins. I know, because I bought a lot of them!

There's been trapping around here for a long time. It was just something farmers did to make a little extra money. At first, they mailed them parcel post to Sears, Roebuck and Company or to fur houses in St. Louis. Later, when buyers got motorized they could travel around the region to buy furs. I've bought 'em on parking lots and front porches all over East Texas. We eventually bought "green" furs and processed them in our fur house. You've got to scrape all those skins to get the fat off and then dry 'em for several days. Then you're ready to ship 'em off to New York City where the brokers are. A lot of my furs traveled by airplane, bundled into bales wrapped in burlap sacking. Once they get to New York, they're kept in cold storage until they're sold by auction or by individual sales to manufacturers. I've even sold them direct to European buyers. Texas 'coons make nice coats with good color. *(He sighs.)*

But all good things gotta end. That's the way it was with the fur trade, at least the one I know about. With the weather getting warmer, people don't need such warm garments. Plus, there were other factors. Some people think it's cruel to kill animals, and others don't like the mess that this kind of business leaves. It's mainly about the environment. I guess we'll all have to become vegetarians. So, the fur trade is largely gone today. But who knows? It may come back, and I plan to be out there buyin' those furs.

(Lights down on Fur Man. Short interlude of a lively dulcimer tune or fiddler playing "Arkansas Traveler.")

S.M.: *(Lights up on S.M.)* A half million raccoon skins! That's more than I can grasp. But, after all, this is Texas where we do things in a big way. Personally, I don't know if I'm ready to buy that vegetarian thing, .. yet. *(He rubs his stomach.)* Back in the late '60s and early '70s, East Texas—like the rest of the country—had its share of people who practiced what they called the "alternative life style." These "hippies," as we called them, wanted to get back to nature in their own way—living in the woods and growing gardens that produced some exotic plants. This next guy knew about all that although he had his own reasons for being a "Hippie."

THE HIPPIE: *(Lights up on a man wearing jeans and a tee shirt and some kind of cap.)* Well, I guess you could call me a Hippie. I opposed the war in Vietnam, and I lived in the woods. Before I came to East Texas in the early 1970s, I got a college degree, took my physical for the draft, and drew a high lottery number. *(Whew!)* Sure, I was against the war, and I even took part in a few protests before I moved here. But I had a job, paid my taxes, and finally grew out of that part of my life.

Hey, I came here because I liked the place. I was looking for a home where I could fish, grow a garden, and enjoy the outdoors. I love the physical beauty of this area. When I'm out there in the outdoors, my concerns just seem to melt away. I try to treat people as I'd want to be treated. Most of the people are A-OK! What's wrong with liking where you live? I'm here to stay!

Sure, we got problems. One of the things that being a Hippie taught me was that you can't judge people by the way they look, and I admit that I looked like heck—long hair, gaudy clothing, and a beard. I got a lot of stares from some people—I could just feel their rejection. That's why I've felt such an affinity with minorities—disliked because you're different. So, I confess that I'm still a rebel at heart. What's wrong with being a maverick? *(He looks at audience with a slight smile and eyes raised.)*

(Lights down on Hippie. Harmonica plays "This Land is Your Land, This Land is My Land.")

S.M.: *(Lights up on S.M.)* I wandered whatever happened to those people. Life is amazing. *(He scratches chin.)* So is death. It's something we don't like to talk about. But it's gonna happen to all of us, folks; that's just the way it is. Death is as natural as birth. We left this next character to nearly the end of our show for obvious reasons: Here's the Undertaker.

THE UNDERTAKER: *(Lights up on a short man in his mid-fifties, dressed in a dark suit, white shirt and tie. He is a jolly man who speaks in a friendly tone.)* I've been in this business for nearly forty years. In fact, I've been knocking around in cemeteries nearly all my life, considering that my grandfather and father were both monument makers. Contrary to what people might think, you have to go to school to learn undertaking. I spent a year in mortuary school down in Houston. We studied chemistry, anatomy, and pathology, and then I had to do a two-year internship. I'd never even attended a funeral before that. Well, I started out with a local funeral home—that's really when I found out what it was all about. Later, I worked for a big mortuary down in the Houston area. My boss was a kind man—he even had to teach me how to dress. After I showed up in a green leisure suit and cowboy boots, he took me to a clothing store and bought me a dark suit and proper shoes. "It's all part of the image," he said.

I also had to learn how to deal with people going through one of the hardest times in anybody's life—the death of a loved one. It's hard to go to the funeral home to make all the plans for a funeral. A lot of you understand what I'm saying. I guess that's why they call us "grief counselors." Now that's a fancy term, but that's exactly what we do. I learned that you have to treat all people the same way, regardless of whether they're rich or poor. You're not a preacher, but you've got to be professional in what you do. You've got to learn that various religious groups treat funerals differently. Some groups show more emotion than others, and you've got to be able to deal with that. You also have to keep your own emotions in check. I can tell you that we all mourn, but we have to be strong for our patrons. For me, the hardest funerals are those involving children. *(He pauses.)*

But you ought to see us at an undertakers' convention. We know how to have fun sharing jokes and experiences. I remember one time when another guy and I were returning the hearse after a run. My friend was driving. I told him to pull into the nearest McDonald's so we could get a Coke. Well, I got in the back of the hearse as we went up to the drive-through, and when the girl took our order, I called out, "The guy back here wants chili beans and a Coke." *(Laughs.)* There's more to being an undertaker than just a somber face and a dark suit, and remember, I'll be the last one to let you down.

(Lights fade as harmonica plays a short rendition of "Nearer, My God to Thee.)

S.M.: *(Lights up on announcer.)* Well, as they say, the old clock on the wall is moving. We've covered a lot of ground thus far in our little journey around the region. Remember the Oldtimer who told us about East Texas in 1900? Well, it's only fair that we conclude with a modern view straight from the mouth of a teenager with an Ipod in one hand and a cell telephone in the other.

THE TEENAGER: *(Young girl—about 17 years old—dances onstage in time with a rock song. She is dressed in modern teenager garb. She eventually calms down enough to talk.)* What's all this history stuff? I don't care to hear about what a bunch of old people did or thought! Like, you know, if it's not happening now, why is it important? *(Phone sounds with a rock song ring; she answers.)* Speak! Oh, hi! *(Listens)* Lunch? Oh, I guess so. See you soon. Bye. See? That was important. Otherwise, I might have had to eat by myself, and that would have been the real pits!

I just love my telephone. *(She bats her eyes)* I can be in touch with anyone anytime. Grown-ups don't understand, but teenagers have to be connected. That's also why we use the Internet so much. Do you realize it's possible to communicate with people virtually anywhere—even overseas? I like to know what other people are doing. Otherwise, how would I know what's happening outside East Texas? Oh, don't get me wrong; I keep up with the news, too—I watch those little lines that crawl along the bottom of the television screen while I'm watching my programs. That tells me pretty much what I need to know.

Now, I realize that a lot of people—my parents and most teachers *(she gives that teenager look)*—they don't think that young people know much. Well, I guess we don't know as much as we should, but it's not our fault. We're so busy going to school and taking tests, we don't have time to learn much. Then, there's drill team, and boys, and clothes. It took me a month to find the right jeans for our trip to Mexico during Spring Break. And, before you know it graduation is here. I don't even know where I'm going to college yet. I'm just too busy! *(Phone sounds)* Hello? *(Listens briefly)* Sure, I can go out tonight. I should be studying for my history test, but it'll be ok. I can study when I get home if I'm not too sleepy. See you about 9. Bye.

(She looks off into space, smiling at audience and returns to seat. Lights down as lively rock song continues.)

S.M.: We've got one more musical act before we get into our finale. I recently heard these ladies on a show right here at the Lamp-Lite. Their music is wonderful, even inspiring. You'll think you've been to Broadway. We are proud to present Mollie and Mary in their rendition of "Hallellujah!" Please welcome Mollie and Mary.

(They set up at microphone and perform.)

S.M.: *(Lights up on S.M. at his microphone.)* Well, that's our show for now, folks. We thank you for coming. Before we leave, I'd like to tell you about an obituary I read in the local paper. It was about a 99-year-old woman from our community who recently died after a long and productive life. She might be like your grandmother or someone else you knew. It seems that one week before she died this woman got a speeding ticket . . . Here's how she might have described it. *(Old woman comes to microphone.)*

MODERN GRANNY: Now, Officer, that wasn't speeding—just driving fast enough to get there on time. Who else is gonna play the hymns for church if I don't get there on time? I've been playing that old piano for 70 years now. Like me, it needs a little tuning, and who's gonna teach that Sunday School class? Are you surprised at me? I taught 40 years in the public schools here—that's three generations of students. Did I teach you, your son, or your daddy? Are you from here? Yep, that's right—three generations of students, and I kept up with the times, I did. Learned to use the computers after I turned 80—taught the "old timers" how to surf the net.

How old am I? Well, how old do you think? How old do I look? Here, take a look at my driver's license—yep, I'm over 90. So you'll let me off with a warning and not a real speeding ticket? And you want me to be careful. Thanks, young man. See you in church.

S.M.: Remarkable. Her obituary ended with her favorite poem by an East Texas poet, Karle Wilson Baker, and that's what we'd like to leave you with today:

*(**TEACHER** reads poem.)*

> "Let me grow lovely, growing old—
>
> So many fine things do:
>
> Laces, and ivory, and gold,
>
> And silks need not be new;
>
> And there is healing in old trees,
>
> Old streets a glamour hold;
>
> Why may not I, as well as these,
>
> Grow Lovely, growing old?"

(As he speaks, appropriate music plays softly in the background; it comes up as he welcomes the cast for a curtain call.)

BOBBY H. JOHNSON was a retired Regents Professor of History at Stephen F. Austin State University. He authored three books: *Wiley Post, His Winnie Mae, and the World's First Pressure Suit* (Washington: Smithsonian Institution and Government Printing Office, 1971), co-authored by Dr. Stanley Mohler; *The Coushatta People* (Phoenix: Indian Tribal Series, 1977.); *A Texas Tragedy: The New London School Explosion A Play in Two Acts* (Nacogdoches: Stephen F. Austin State University Press, 2012.) Additionally, he compiled and edited a series of interviews, *From Pine Trees to Paper: Interviews with Southland Paper Employees* (Center for East Texas Studies, Stephen F. Austin State University, 2002).

In 2008, Dr. Johnson received the Life-time Achievement Award from the Texas Oral History Association for his collection of several hundred interviews, primarily on East Texas, which are held by the East Texas Research Center at Stephen F. Austin State University. These plays, a result of these many interviews, were presented at the Lamp-Lite Theater from 1991 through 2009, and one was performed in February 2020. He held an M.A. (University of Oklahoma School of Journalism, 1962) and a Ph.D. in history from the University of Oklahoma (1967). He taught history at Stephen F. Austin State University from 1966 to 2005. He was married to Myrna E. Johnson, and they lived in Nacogdoches, TX. They have two daughters, both teachers, and four grandchildren. Although Bobby had Alzheimers disease, he passed away from COVID-19.

www.ingramcontent.com/pod-product-compliance
Lightning Source LLC
Chambersburg PA
CBHW030526080526
44586CB00011B/332